Marcus Berkmann has spent more than thirty years sitting in front of various television screens swearing at incompetent England batsmen. For the past twenty-five of them he has also run a travelling cricket team, founded at Oxford and now conducting itself with appropriate lack of decorum at scenic village grounds across the country. In his leisure time he writes columns on pop music for the *Spectator* and films for the *Oldie*, and has written columns on sport for the *Independent on Sunday*, *Punch* and the *Daily Express*. His lifetime batting average (boosted by several recent not outs) is a whisker under 5.4.

'Enjoy a spell of obsessive indulgence in the company of a genuine and witty enthusiast'   *The Times*

'It captures splendidly the many dazzling facets of the truly atrocious cricketer'   *Observer*

'For addicts with a low batting average – i.e. most cricket lovers'   *Guardian*

'An intensely amusing piece of work, which will delight anyone who has ever been caught by his wife in the act of playing an imaginary cover drive in the bathroom mirror' Harry Thompson

Also by Marcus Berkmann

BRAIN MEN: A PASSION TO COMPETE

Rain Men

THE MADNESS OF CRICKET

Marcus Berkmann

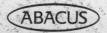

An *Abacus* Book

First published in Great Britain by Little, Brown 1995
This edition published by Abacus 1996
Reprinted 1996, 1997 (twice), 1999, 2000, 2001, 2002, 2003, 2004

A CIP catalogue record for this book
is available from the British Library.

ISBN 0 349 10742 4

Printed and bound in England by Clays Ltd, St Ives plc

Abacus
An imprint of
Time Warner Book Group UK
Brettenham House
Lancaster Place
London WC2E 7EN

www.twbg.co.uk

Contents

Acknowledgements

This book was the idea of Richard Beswick and Alan Samson at Little, Brown: to both I owe considerable gratitude. Thanks also to my fellow Captain Scott founders Terence Russoff, Harry Thompson and Richard Corden, all of whom suggested good ideas and/or read early drafts; and for unwittingly supplying so much material my Captain Scott comrades Cliff Allen, Stephen Arkell, Mark Brisenden, Tim Cooper, Arvind Dewan, Martin Dyckhoff, Matthew Greenburgh, Bill 'Chariots of Fire' Hoath, Patrick Howarth, Joe Hunter, David Jaques, Bob Jones, Howard McMinn, Cie Malde, Bill Matthews, Steve Mills, Peter Momtchiloff, Chris Moore, Andy Morse, Francis Peckham, Neal Ransome, Colin Schindler, Ian Wall, the late Brian Warr, Charlie Williams and all the other frauds, bores and deadbeats who have infested the team over the years. Thanks also to Andy Robson, Nick Newman and Jane Parbury for all those dismal days at Test matches; to David Thomas and Simon O'Hagan for hiring me; and to Matthew Burrows, Keren Martin, Elisabeth Reissner, Kate Saunders, Phil South, David Taylor, Patrick Walsh and Philip Wells for their advice and encouragement.

Introduction

August 1994. Another beautiful summer morning. Loads of work to do. Important not to let the day dribble away. But first I check Ceefax to confirm that Graham Gooch will be fit for tomorrow's Test match. I ring a couple of regulars who play for my own team to confirm that they are still on for Saturday's game, only to find that one isn't back from holiday yet and the other is in a meeting until lunchtime. I practise my pull shot in front of the drawing-room mirror with a ruler. I read the cricket reports in two newspapers. I check Ceefax again.

There are many of us, and we are all the same. At some cathartic moment in our stunted childhoods, this ridiculous sport inveigled itself into our consciousnesses like a virus, and never left. Now we stumble cheerfully through life, performing normal tasks and living relatively normal lives, while at the back of our minds a small but insistent question lurks. What's the Test score? You can see it in the faces of men everywhere, whether coerced into purchasing DIY equipment on Saturday afternoons by unforgiving spouses, or rushing home at the end of a hard day's toil to catch the last seven minutes of play on BBC2. What's the Test score? And that's just the beginning of it. Find out the Test score, and you have to know more. Who got the wickets? Does this radio pick up long wave? Are England all out yet?

There are many of us. I suppose it's some consolation. We are everywhere, and we speak freely of our obsession, as long as our wives and girlfriends aren't in the room. But it was not always like this. When we were younger, we had to be altogether more circumspect about our feelings. At my school, football was pre-eminent. It was the national sport. To be obsessed by football was considered natural, even wholesome. Football was a man's game, involving mud, cold, random violence and, if you were really lucky, serious injury. For the British boy on the threshold of man's estate, football supplied every rite of accession that anyone might reasonably need.

Cricket never had the same cachet. Cricket was played during the summer, itself a girly time of year, and the shortage of mud and homoerotic physical contact did not exactly enhance its appeal to the more dedicated sportsmen. Besides, cricket relied too much on fripperies like the weather and the state of the pitch. Footballers didn't give a stuff about the weather, and the nastier the state of the pitch, the happier they were.

In youth, the urge to conform is all but irresistible. Each of us grew up convinced that he was the only person who felt this way. We turned first to the cricket scores, but only when no one was looking. This strange urge to wear long white trousers and a multi-coloured cap . . . well, it's not natural, is it? So we kept quiet about our true devotions, and adopted the ingenious camouflage of the football fanatic. When I was at school, I accepted willingly that Ted Hemsley was a gritty central defender, and stalwart of the Sheffield United side of the early 1970s. But when I was at home, clutching my secret copy of *Wisden*, I acknowledged what I knew to be true: that E.J.O. Hemsley was a gritty middle-order batsman for Worcestershire, and occasional medium-pace bowler.

Only as we approached adulthood did we realise that we were not in fact alone; that out there, in the footballing wastelands, small pockets of cricketing resistance thrived. In the late 1970s, when I was in my teens, we identified each other by means of certain codewords dropped art-lessly into the conversation. Sitting in pubs with fellow undergraduates, trying to work out whether these would be the friends for life we had heard about, or merely passing acquaintances whose company we would forever avoid after this evening, we would chat around all the usual subjects, expressing a learned opinion on the latest single by The Dooleys, perhaps, or the new series of *Bless This House* – and then, while no one was really paying attention, we would slip in our codewords ('Little Harry Pilling') and wait to see if anyone took notice. Often these hallowed syllables would fall on stony ground; but occasionally someone would look up from his drink with a start, unable to believe what he thought he had just heard. Did someone say 'Little Harry Pilling'? Could there be someone else in the world who knew that J.W.H.T. Douglas was the only England captain ever to have four initials? By dropping into the general chat an equally ingenious set of coded responses ('That was four from the moment it left the bat'), your new friend could indicate that he too was of the cricketing persuasion. Thus were formed bonds that have lasted to this day.

Over the months, many more of us 'emerged from the cupboard', as we liked to put it, as our cupboards were where we hid our secret hoards of *The Cricketer* and linseed oil. Soon we were all meeting in covert groups to exchange Colin Dredge anecdotes or discuss the strange inability of Trevor Jesty to get into the England team. The football boys thought we were out of our minds, reluctant as we were to wear brightly coloured scarves and kick each other to death all winter long. What they thought we got up to in our meetings doesn't bear thinking about. But as anyone who has tried it knows, real games of Howzat take hours to play.

In adulthood, you somehow expect to recover from all this. You assume that, as youthful zeal fades, the grim drudgery of daily life will supersede all such nonsense. But it doesn't happen. Your obsession remains as vivid as ever. For once cricket has claimed you, it never lets you go. Sooner or later you simply have to accept that England's results matter, whether or not you want them to. The day after

England were out for 46 in the West Indies, I sat in a pub with a friend and seriously discussed selling my flat, giving up all my freelance work and going abroad for a couple of years to write unpublishable novels about the artist's inner struggle. A week later England won and I decided that it would be more fun just to have a party. There is no logic behind any of this. Nowadays I can remember little of what I learned at school and absolutely nothing of what I read at university, but I do know, off the top of my head, that Sir Donald Bradman scored 6,996 Test runs, and was out second ball for 0 in his final innings (bowled Hollies), thus losing the opportunity to end his Test career with an average of 100. One old friend of mine, who for security reasons cannot be identified, used to have terrible problems remembering the PIN numbers for his various bank cards, and was always having them forcibly reclaimed by machines, until he was given the opportunity to set his own PIN number and chose the only number he knew he would always remember – Clive Lloyd's Test aggregate of 7,515. Having regularly removed large amounts of money from his account, I can confirm that he keeps the number to this day.

This book is for all such obsessives. It's for anyone who has sat hour after hour in front of Ceefax while BBC2 shows Wimbledon. It's for the weekend player who happily gives up his valuable afternoon to be given out for 0 by an umpire who can't quite remember the lbw law; for the couch potato who bought cable or satellite purely because BSkyB had the rights to Tests overseas; for the sensualist who, in the middle of winter, goes to sports shops to try out bats without the remotest intention of buying one. It's for the motorway driver who listens to *Test Match Special* and narrowly avoids crashing whenever someone takes a wicket. It's for anyone who has ever blubbed at a video of Botham's Ashes. There are many of us, and we are all the same.

CHAPTER ONE

A Matter of Faith

The great question is: why? Why cricket? Why not tenpin bowling or darts? A year or so ago I was at a children's party, surreptitiously watching the Test match in the spare bedroom on a portable black-and-white TV, far away from the blancmange-spattered mêlée. Not quite far enough, however, for just as the match was getting exciting, a four-year-old walked in and asked me what I was doing. I was watching the cricket, I explained.

'Why?'

'Because I like it.'

'Why?'

Precocious little bastard. A moment later my then girl-friend walked in. 'Yes, why do you like cricket?' she said, scenting blood. 'I think it's boring,' said the repellent infant. 'So do I,' said my soon-to-be-ex-girlfriend. I was cornered. Why? Why? Why?

It is a question that arises time and time again. Non-believers cannot understand how anyone could allow themselves to fall under the spell of a mere game, and such an intrinsically silly one at that. Their sneers and contempt, not to mention their endless satirical use of the phrase 'bowling a maiden over', can undermine the most robust of personalities. What they don't understand is that we know it's stupid, but England are 82 for 4, for Christ's sake. Which, needless to say, answers all their questions in full.

If really pushed for a response, I talk of cricket's grace, its physical bravery, its psychological and intellectual dimensions, its emotional resonances, of the confrontation between batsman and bowler, of the struggle for power, the endless possibilities, the unpredictable flux. After four hours' detailed (some might say definitive) advocacy, sometimes with the use of audio-visual aids and always with a complete description of the various grips a leg-spinner might use, I tiptoe out of the room before my unwitting audience wakes up.

But how can you hope to justify it? Cricket is a matter of faith. Either you believe, or you don't believe. There is no rational explanation. In discussing our hopeless enslavement to the sport, we have to talk in abstract, even devotional terms if we are to make any sense of it at all. Perhaps cricket is more than a sport. Perhaps funda-mentalist religion would be a more accurate description.

Dead though he may be, I think the Ayatollah Khomeini

would know where we were coming from. He would think we were wrong, but he would admire the style of our wrongness. Cricket leaves no room for doubt. Its superiority as a sport is manifest. If the heathens cannot accept this, they cannot really argue if we have them horribly put to death. The problem is that British cricket fans are such a meek lot. There we are, always having to justify ourselves to cynical girlfriends and four-year-olds possessed by Satan. We smile politely as idiots pull out those teatowels that purport to explain the laws of cricket by endless satirical repetition of the words 'in' and 'out'. The Mujaheddin would not stand for this. Just a glimpse of a teatowel parodying the Koran and the death squads would be let loose. We could learn from this.

The more you think about it, the more attractive the idea of Cricket As Religion becomes. After all, we already have all the trappings. We have the devilishly complex theology, whose baroque byways confuse even the most dedicated adherents. We have the curious vestments, for white is a holy colour in many religions. We have our holy book, published each April in both hardback and paperback editions. We have our priestly caste, the self-styled 'first-class' cricketers who sacrifice all for their chosen vocation, bar the odd sponsored car. For matters of doctrinal policy, we can consult God's own representative on earth, the chairman of selectors. God even turns up in person from time to time, pronouncing from on high (BBC2) that his grandmother could have caught that in her pinny. Good grief, we even play the game on Sundays.

And like all the most entertaining religions, there's none

of this wishy-washy liberal nonsense to cloud the minds of the faithful. Shi'ite Muslims could take a few tips from the laws of cricket, which allow for no interpretation, no leeway. A true believer knows, more utterly than he know the names of his wife and three children, that if the ball pitches outside leg, he cannot be lbw. There can be no appeal against this ruling. The laws are fixed forever, or at least until the next meeting of the ICC.

Faith in such absolutes is not easily mocked. You don't mess with the fundamental laws of nature. No man may venture into the corridor of uncertainty, for, as the prophets say, hang your bat out to dry and you will probably be caught behind. We understand that. We draw strength from our understanding. Unlike a few lily-livered religions I could name, we have no room in cricket for doubt or equivocation. Anglicans may *believe* that Christ was resurrected after death, but we *know* that David Gower should have gone to India in 1992–3.

We proselytise. We don't necessarily mean to, but we can't help it. We get married, we have sons, we teach them to hold a bat before they can walk. On their fourth birthdays, we lead them into the garden where a makeshift net has been erected, and we bowl inswinging leg-cutters at them until they pass out with tiredness. They take up tennis or shot-putting and we disinherit them.

We have moments of revelation. Perhaps once, when we were children, we did not believe at all. Perhaps we were too busy with our homework, or just engaging in the random cruelty and violence that customarily dominates the lives of small boys. Then one day we were playing tip-and-run in the playground, or maybe even watching a one-day match on television, when a blinding light suddenly enveloped the land, and a male voice did speak, and it was pregnant with authority, and it was probably Richie Benaud, and he said 'Morning, everyone,' and life was never the same again. Don't think you are special: it happens to us all.

Anyone who really seeks an answer to the Great Question, of course, need go no further than London NW8. Eventually every believer must make his own pilgrimage to Lord's. For centuries cricketing theologians have debated the significance of this mythic rectangle. Once again, though, it is the language that gives it away. Lord's is the 'cradle' of cricket. No other ground could be said to have a 'nursery' end. Or, if you prefer a more exotic parallel, Lord's has also long been known as cricket's Mecca. Many times I have felt an overwhelming desire to heed the call of the muezzin and kneel down in the direction of St John's Wood. It is a holy place, where the faithful foregather. When another England batsman is out for 0, the hush around the ground has an almost spiritual intensity. Barging through the angry crowd at teatime, queuing for a watery beer, perhaps even slipping up on an escaped hot dog, you can never quite overcome your sheer relief that you are there, at the centre of it all. I myself am happiest when the ground is completely deserted, such as on the final day of a very exciting County Championship match. In empty stands, gaggles of pensioners nibble on curled sandwiches. Sad men in parkas score every ball in rapt silence. In the pavilion, men in MCC ties eat huge lunches, unaware that any cricket is being played

at all. And yet the dignity and splendour of Lord's remain
intact. William Blake was never terribly precise about his
assertion that Jerusalem was built here in England's green
and pleasant land, but if he had had an A–Z to hand, I
think he might have discovered it a brisk walk from Baker
Street tube station.

Yes, cricket would make a fine religion (I particularly
look forward to the holy wars against golf). What cricket
has to offer is the full gamut of emotional and intellectual
experience, adding pain to pleasure and having much to
say on the concept of Triumph Through Adversity. It may
actually do us good to watch England fail over and over
again. And yet we never stop believing that, against all
the evidence, one day they might succeed. For in cricket,
absolute faith is compatible with absolute cynicism. God is
the ultimate umpire, and He's waiting to saw you off.

CHAPTER TWO

Captain Scott

From watching cricket, thinking about cricket, talking about cricket and reading about cricket, it's but a short step to the ultimate of time-wasters, playing cricket. In 1979 I couldn't get a game with my college side at university, on the (I thought) spurious grounds that I was not good enough. Not good enough? I wasn't even that good, having only twice played outside my back garden. At school only those who showed a natural aptitude for the game were allowed anywhere near a cricket pitch. Tuition was deemed necessary only for those who didn't need it. The rest of us were sent on cross-country runs across the scenic mud swamps of Hampstead Heath, which usually claimed at least two lives per term. To be fat, short or

unconscionably weedy at my school (I qualified under the
second and third categories) was to renounce all claim to
human rights, which included officially sanctioned access to
cricket. It was heartbreaking. Every Wednesday afternoon,
as we were led screaming to our weekly brush with death,
we would pass the First XI as they prepared for another
leisurely 40-over friendly on the billiard-table perfection
of Senior Field, watched by admiring long-limbed lovelies
from the locals girls' school. How vividly are the cruel
inequalities of adolescence illustrated. Later on, most of
these rangy athletes would grow fat and become estate
agents, advertising their sad little companies in the school's
old boys' magazine. At the time, however, such sublime
twists of fate seemed beyond hope. A quick end in the
quagmire near Kenwood House was as much as we could
hope for.

   I survived. Unfortunately, just as the victims of failed
relationships always seem to pursue exactly the same sort
of person who let them down before, so I ended up at
an Oxford college full of natural athletes bristling with a
well-developed contempt for sporting incompetents. Most
of the First XI seemed to be challenging for Blues, while
the traditional 'joke' cricket team was the province of
overmuscled rowers with huge jaws and inconceivably
blonde girlfriends. In the bar, people drank testosterone
by the pint. Even the girls seemed to be on steroids. There
was no place for me here.

   So, in a fit of pique, I and three like-minded friends
started our own team. The worms had turned. Who
were these firm-thighed mesomorphs to tell us whether

we could play cricket or not? Surely there was a role for the athletically challenged, for the thin and the unco-ordinated, for the partially sighted, the overweight and the inert? The folly of our ambition had an almost heroic quality, so we christened our team the Captain Scott Invitation XI, in honour of the intrepid polar explorer. In later years, some of us have come to regret this whimsical undergraduate gesture, especially those who have sought to turn us into a 'real' cricket team, whatever that is. Even so, I think we chose our role model well. No one could ever fault Scott for his extraordinary courage. His ideas were big; it was just his brain that was small. Even in 1910, when he embarked on his final doomed expedition to the South Pole, it was established practice to use huskies to transport equipment. Scott therefore chose to use horses, which all died. He was history's greatest runner-up, a leader of men who, tragically, led them to their death. Reading his journals in the library, I was greatly moved by the fearless rigidity of his upper lip, a condition that the weather in the Antarctic can only have augmented. In the end he failed pitifully, but at least he failed in the right spirit. 'Had we lived,' he wrote, 'I should have had a tale to tell of the hardihood, endurance and courage of my companions which would have stirred the heart of every Englishman. These rough notes and our dead bodies must tell the tale.' It was much as we felt in our first season, as we lost game after game after game.

Anyone who starts a cricket team does so in a spirit of hope, dreaming of glory and heroic feats. Then you lose your first umpteen matches. Those early days saw us destroyed by a succession of sides ranging from the mediocre to the barely competent. We were hopeless. Our kit, bought on the cheap, began to fall apart within weeks, while our personnel proved if anything even less sturdy. We tried out players from all over the university. Many played once, and then left messages to say that they had contracted rare tropical diseases, or had been called out of the country on urgent family business. Early team photos show several players with beards whom no one can now identify. Most have that look of dulled terror you see on the faces of laboratory beagles who smoke forty cigarettes a day. Our gravest loss was someone called Tim, who owned a Range Rover. One day he just disappeared, and we all had to take the bus.

But as this first traumatic season continued, a few regulars did emerge. My old schoolfriend Harry, who ran the team with me, was an all-rounder of little obvious ability but frightening determination. My college friends Terence and Richard also filled vital roles: Terence owned a Mini, and Richard was the only person in the team who had ever played properly before. We therefore made him captain, which was a mistake. His deep knowledge of cricket did not extend to an ability to inspire and instruct a team of novices. In our first game Terence and Richard opened the batting, and both reached double figures. Marvellous, we thought, an established opening partnership. This was mistake number two: Terence's 13 turned out to be his highest score for six years. He now bats at number 11, and even that sometimes seems a little high.

That first game, against the Oxfordshire village of Bladon, was almost a blueprint for the future, as it saw a number of Captain Scott traditions unwittingly initiated. Having managed to rustle up a mere ten players, we borrowed a sub from the other side, a Mr Owen Gritt, who dropped three dolly catches and was out first ball. Bladon scored 250 for 4, their opener making 127 not out, having been out for 0 in all his previous innings that season. Our bowling was magnanimous. Opening with Harry was a worryingly hip medical student called Tom Cairns, who had said at our first team meeting that he could 'bowl a bit'. Mistake number three. Never listen to anyone who says he can 'bowl a bit'. It either means that he has recently bowled out a State side in Australia, or that he will bowl an average of 7 wides an over. Tom Cairns had a plausible manner and a sharp haircut, so we took him at his word, and in that first season his bowling average was 102.

Our batting, despite that encouraging first-wicket partnership, proved fragile. After Terence was out, swishing frantically across the line, he came back to umpire, and gave Richard out lbw to a ball that pitched six inches outside leg stump. As Terence disappeared into the trees, chased by the irate batsman, Scott collapsed from 53 for 2 to 63 all out. Five batsmen were out for 0, while I began a historic sequence of strokeless 0 not outs that, occasionally interrupted by a real 0, continues to this day.

Over the next three summers we played an average of a dozen games a season against college teams and nearby villages. Most of those we lost. As Harry later wrote of a typical game against Balliol Erratics, 'The Scott batting crumbled like a wholemeal biscuit under a ton of concrete.' More regulars emerged: a mysterious Balkan physicist from

Yorkshire, who became the first in a long string of official best players; Chris Moore, whose endless moaning and frantic self-justification quickly endeared him to his new team-mates; his old schoolfriend Neal Ransome, then in the midst of growing a horrible student beard; and Matthew Greenburgh, whose gargantuan self-confidence very nearly concealed a striking shortage of talent. Of these only Neal still plays. Tom Cairns was one of the first to disappear, seduced by the glory of student theatre and also, we suspected, embarrassed by the fact that none of us had haircuts quite as sharp as his. But his name lives on. Each year at our dinner the Tom Cairns Award is presented to the bowler who has recorded the worst bowling average throughout the season. In sixteen years, no one has ever managed to beat that 102.

When we left university, we took the team with us, and now play thirty-five or so games a season, all 'friendlies', in various cricketing outposts in the south of England. We remain a mixed-ability side, not least because otherwise I would never get a game. Harry, whose dedication remains absolute, has transformed himself into a reliable medium-pace bowler and an obdurate opening batsman. Terence now has a company Ford Sierra. Richard has not captained for years, and now concentrates on playing innings of peerless elegance in which he never seems to score more than 8. Harry captains on Saturday and I captain on Sunday. We still just play for the fun of it, and we still often come humiliatingly second.

The miracle is that it has lasted so long. What began as merely a gesture of defiance has become an important part of our lives. Over the years, new stalwarts have emerged: Francis, our high-flying merchant banker, whose fascination with death and torture is translated into a violent batting style somewhat at odds with his otherwise placid appearance; Arvind, our lubricious solicitor from Delhi, well practised in the ancient art of running out team-mates without a flicker of self-reproach; and Tim, our perennially angry fast bowler. Tim is a tabloid reporter whose wife is a psychologist, which may eventually make him one of the longest and most detailed case studies in psychological history. He is always convinced that the other team is cheating, especially when he's been bowled first ball for the fourth match in succession. Last season, when one opposing team was fifteen minutes late, he suggested, without irony, that we go round to their houses and 'do them over'.

Other players have long since disappeared. The mysterious Balkan left when his status as official best player was undermined by a catastrophic loss of form. Matthew Greenburgh decreed that to play cricket over the age of thirty was absurdly undignified, which, considering how bad he was, was probably true. Chris Moore lasted longest, whingeing in the outfield, complaining on his way to the crease, at the crease, on his way back from the crease. It was as though he saw the endless fruitless games of cricket we played as some sort of metaphor for the inescapable meaninglessness of modern existence, although some players thought he was just a pain in the arse. Eventually he married an Italian woman in his usual truculent manner, and gloomily moved to Milan. A few years ago I spotted him there in a café, and he gave me a look so unambiguously hostile that I felt compelled to wander up and say hello. Age, I discovered, had not withered his ill temper, nor custom staled his infinite ennui.

So we flourish, and our batting still collapses, and Terence still gives people out when the ball has pitched outside leg stump 'because it was going to hit the wicket'. Captain Scott now occupies about half of my cricketing life. One side of my brain concentrates on the first-class game, or the way cricket should be played. The other deals with the way cricket really is played. Through a combination of the two, you can spend virtually your whole life in a haze of cricket. Everything else passes in a flash. Cricketing agnostics habitually accuse us of using the game to blot out the more painful and difficult aspects of life. But what can be more painful and difficult than a cricket season? The knuckle on my left hand has never been the same since that dropped catch last August. It's not that cricket is a substitute for real life. It *is* real life. It's realer than real life. Psychosis, Tim's wife calls it.

CHAPTER THREE

March

It is a glorious day, the first truly beautiful day of spring. Bright sunlight pours through your window while outside, on budding trees, photogenic songbirds warble joyous tunes. You can feel the adrenaline surging through your veins. For, as Tennyson so sagely wrote (and was subsequently so misquoted), in the spring a young man's fancy turns lightly to thoughts of cricket. The world is waking up after the long winter, and so are you. You stare out of the window, dreaming of battling half-centuries and instinctive diving catches at deep gully.

Self-delusion starts early in the cricket season. Bright sunny March days are one of God's cruellest tricks, for they promise so much and deliver so little. From within it all looks so inviting. But, should you make the mistake of venturing outside without thermal long johns and four pairs of socks, you will surely suffer the consequences, as local authority workmen have to be called out to chip you from the pavement.

Any thoughts of playing cricket are therefore out of the question, unless you fancy a new career as an ice sculpture. Fortunately there's nothing to stop you thinking about cricket, so you think about it all day long. March is the month of hope and dreams, of optimism and anticipation, of long-term memory loss. By the time March rolls along you have completely forgotten how disastrous last season was. Every batting failure and dropped catch have been eradicated by five months of cricket-free complacency. Some scientists blame central heating. Nor should you underestimate the mind-addling effects of all those cosy cricket books you got for Christmas. Now, watching the TV highlights of England's overseas tour, you begin to think that perhaps cricket isn't such a hard game after all. If Alec Stewart can do it, why can't you? They say that cricket is played in the mind, but never more so than this.

And so, befuddled by the deceitful gleam of the chilly March sun, you grab your trusty ruler and play the first of thousands of forward defensives in front of your bedroom mirror. All things considered, it's remarkably easy to time the ball with a ruler. Suddenly you hear a distant rumble and you're at the crease, padded, helmeted, ruler in hand, as Curtly Ambrose storms in from the horizon and the Sabina Park crowd bay for Anglo-Saxon blood. Typical that the sightscreen should be too low at that end. How are you supposed to see the ball coming out of his hand? But then you can only blame yourself if he's a little fired up. You really shouldn't have hit his last ball for 4. Three slips and 2 gullys await as he roars in towards the crease. He bowls. You can barely see it, it's viciously swift, but hang on, it's a little short . . . and wide . . . and luckily the pitch has eased a little this morning, and you're seeing the ball like a basketball, so you rock back, watching it all the way to the sweet spot, and you don't feel a thing, and it rockets away to the point boundary. A huge cheer from the crowd – they love a good contest. The man down there didn't have a chance. You glance round. Richie Richardson at first slip is shaking his head in despair. They had the match virtually won before you came in. You almost feel sorry for him. But don't get cocky. Your 50 may be on the board, but the team needs a big 100 from you. Concentrate. Don't relax for a moment. Do that silly eye exercise Robin Smith showed you. But Ambrose is back, and this time he overpitches, and you lean effortlessly into the ball – ping. Lots of red marks on the centre of your bat today. Whoosh through extra cover, past the fielder's outstretched right hand, and straight into the advertising hoarding before you finish your first run. And all this after you dismissed Brian Lara for 0 with your first ball of the day. Man of the match? Man of the series, more like . . .

Then you wake up, and it's March again. Richie Benaud is always droning on about light bats, but perhaps someone should tell him how potent a well-balanced ruler can be in the right hands. It's just a shame you are not so fluent when holding a real bat. Mirror cricket has these advantages and more over the normal game. There's little chance of injury, although I did bang my head on the door last winter while expertly hooking Wasim Akram for 6. And it takes up so much less time: I have found that I can fantasise a complete Test match in a little over twenty minutes. Cricket may be realer than real life, but never underestimate the power of the imagination. In real life I am a deeply pedestrian right-handed batsman, slow of reaction, limited of shot (forward defensive) and liable to get out for 1. In the mirror I am a dashing left-hander, not unlike David Gower, elegant and unflappable. Once the real cricket season starts, the unstoppable momentum of real-life failure renders all such fantasies impossible. Only in March can you enjoy so vivid and productive a cricketing career. Only in March can you dream that you have taken 6 for 34 on the final morning of a Test against Australia, and then wake deliriously happy at four o'clock in the morning, convinced for five or even six seconds that it actually happened.

And so you potter cheerfully about, digging up rank-smelling old kit from wherever you buried it for environmental reasons last September, playing mirror cricket, ringing up friends and discussing which of the teams you played last year have told you they never want to see you again, all that sort of thing. I think this is where we can most accurately sort the cricket-mad sheep from the half-hearted sporting goats. While the goats are still playing football, the sheep will spend hours fondling battered old cricket balls and hand-washing cricket sweaters that shrank in a thunderstorm last year and so can't be worn anyway. The sheep wash and iron all their cricket shirts weeks in advance, while the work shirts they have to wear tomorrow languish in the dirty washing basket. It's a matter of keeping things in proportion. The season begins in five weeks and six days, and we want to be ready.

My own favourite ritual is the cleaning of the box, which has almost certainly lain untouched for months at the bottom of the miniature ecosystem otherwise known as my cricket bag. This small and undistinguished implement is going to protect my reproductive organs for the next five months, so it seems only fair to keep it in good nick. Lovingly I soap it and rinse it, perhaps adding a layer of Pledge for that all-weather gonad-guarding shine. You can overdo it, of course: one year I used so many different detergents and fluids on it that the damn thing started to melt.

More prosperously proportioned players can also play the Great Trouser Game, for a decision about last year's whites must be made sooner or later. Option 1: Sooner. Try them on now. If they are too small, at least there is still a chance of buying a replacement pair at a reasonable cost, before the full-season prices have taken hold. Option 2: Later. This choice, while less practical, gives you another month of fooling yourself that you are the same weight you were last year. If you haven't tried them on, they can't yet be too small. Besides, if you tried them on now and just managed to squeeze into them, what is the guarantee that you will be quite as svelte in six weeks' time, when you actually have to play? Far easier to delay the decision and keep your pride intact.

What is crucial, though, is not to delay the decision too long, for the Great Trouser Game carries a fearsome booby prize. The first game of the season arrives, and you somehow cram yourself into your old trousers. Team-mates make ribald comments about sardines. You can still move freely. Just don't try any sudden breathing. You saunter out to the pitch. No problems yet. You run around a bit. Not a hint of structural damage. But then the ball is hit past you, and you run off to retrieve it, and as you bend over to pick it up, a huge, rasping comedy tearing noise is heard across much of the surrounding countryside. Your multi-coloured boxer shorts have been revealed to an amused populace. Peals of merry laughter ring out at your expense. This is the Fat Cricketer's Nightmare, and it's happening to you.

As a thin person myself, I can't really understand why anyone would let himself get into such a scrape, but then cricketing fatties seem more prone than most to attacks of self-delusion. 'Fat? I'm not fat!' they cry, inadvertently knocking you flying with one or other of their extraneous mounds of flab. And so the start of every new season inevitably resounds to the crowd-pleasing clamour of ripping trousers, as half a year's non-stop eating wreaks its bitter revenge.

But that is a joy to come. For now, the thrill of anticipation overwhelms all lesser sensibilities, like hunger and tiredness. Even when the brief sunny spell comes to its usual stormy close, I feel undaunted by the month-long wait before things really get going. For in my mind's eye, Shane Warne is coming round the wicket, whipping his arm over, but the ball didn't come out from behind his hand, and it's short, and it's the flipper, and I ease back with bat straight and defend and *plock*! straight into the middle of the bat. And

Warne pulls that face, that nearly-had-you-that-time look of his, but this one is overpitched, and I dance up the wicket and catch it on the full and caress it past mid-on's flailing fingers for a magnificent 4 and is that my 100? Good Lord, it is – and I remove my helmet and raise my bat and smile for the TV cameras. And the announcer comes over the PA and reveals to the ecstatic multitude that I have now scored over 1,000 Test runs in a calendar year for the third time, and it's only July . . .

CHAPTER FOUR

In the Village

The time for painful truths has arrived. Much of this book is concerned with the customs and practices of village cricket, a form of the game that, over the years, has received only the most favourable press. First-class and international cricket have been tainted by gamesmanship, accusations of cheating and Merv Hughes' moustache. Village cricket, by contrast, remains unsullied by commercialism, and is generally felt to have kept alive the game's more honourable traditions. Indeed, to the vast majority of non-participants, the mere mention of the words 'village' and 'cricket' instantly conjures up a sepia-toned rustic idyll, full of burly blacksmiths and wily off-spinning parsons, and chaps with pipes called Jack, who always score 100 in even time but never hit across the line. Robin redbreasts tweet from the branches of 200-year-old oaks, while floppy-eared bunny rabbits scamper cutely through the undergrowth. No four-lane bypasses soil the perimeter of this little paradise. There are no day-trippers, no New Age travellers, no twenty-five-year-old suits from the City buying up all the best houses in the village as holiday homes. Nor are there licensing hours this glorious summer Sunday, for the jolly pub landlord is still dispensing foaming tankards of strong local ale at 4.30 pm. Yokels in smocks, lambs bleating, small children in sailor suits, etc. etc. etc.

What a cosy vision. What elemental, prelapsarian innocence. What total bollocks. When Adam and Eve left the Garden of Eden, they didn't absentmindedly forget to take village cricket with them. And yet, despite the weekly efforts of thousands of enthusiastic village players, this nauseating image continues to prevail. I blame decades of black propaganda from the *Test Match Special* team, not to mention all those dismal TV costume dramas which use village cricket matches as scenic backdrops for their own feeble storylines.

'Ar, Seth, great days. The harvest's in, young Sir Basil's to get wed, and now his Lordship is 50 not out against Piddlingfold. Well played, your Lordship! Ar, Seth, we'll never see days like this again.'

'Ar, Josh, that we won't. Fancy another foaming tankard of strong local ale?'

Twenty minutes later, Seth and Josh are mown down by machine-gun fire at Mons.

The image prevails, moreover, because certain people

wish it to prevail. Advertisers keen to make their worthless products appear more 'rural'. Unscrupulous publishers shamelessly reprinting terrible old cricket books from the 1930s. Tim Rice. The list is endless. But whoever may ultimately be responsible, the result is that millions of innocent Britons believe that village cricket has been magically preserved from some golden age of sport to represent all that was once fine and fair about our great nation, before the twentieth century barged in and ruined everything.

The truth, needless to say, is rather less palatable. Never in many hundreds of village cricket matches have I ever seen a floppy-eared bunny rabbit scamper anywhere, unless it's under the wheel of a passing lorry. Robin redbreasts search in vain for branches of 200-year-old oaks from which to tweet, as Farmer Giles plc has had them all cut down. The last burly blacksmith died in 1967. The jolly landlord waters down his Skol. The new parson spends Saturday afternoons with his close friend Clive. And the game is anything but a soft-focus backdrop to a TV costume drama. Village cricket is a brutal sport in which the strong thrive and the weak are quickly pummelled into submission. Some observers compare it to cock-fighting. I think bear-baiting would be nearer the mark. The outsider sees only elegant white figures bounding across the picturesque village green, cheerfully yelling expletives at each other. But beneath that calm idyllic surface, raging torrents surge.

For, as so often in cricket, there is a yawning gap between the way things are and the way people would like them to be. People see what they want to see, and they would rather see village cricket than watch it. It is their choice to miss the subtleties of play, the artful stratagems, the blatant cheating and the random violence.

Let us be blunt: opposing teams will do virtually anything to nobble each other. Tactical use of partially sighted umpires; stomach-deadening teas; donkey-drop bowlers bowling out of the late afternoon sun; scoreboard 'foul-ups'; ball-switching; double-headed coins; far better players: no subterfuge is too low to see regular employment in the moral vacuum of the village game.

Much of this needle is geographic in origin: neighbouring villages consumed by mutual loathing, neighbouring towns consumed by mutual loathing, neighbouring counties consumed by mutual loathing. North versus south, rural versus suburban. Old versus young, young versus younger. Disraeli would never have spoken of One Nation if he had played village cricket. Class is also a familiar battleground. Village lads in their capped-sleeve T-shirts hang out by the telephone box, muttering 'Bloody yuppies' as the visiting stockbrokers drive past in their company BMWs.

And yet the needle between the teams is merely the start of the hostilities, the first rumble of gunfire before everyone pours over the top into the fray. Most spectators at village matches probably assume, not unreasonably, that cricketers are primarily concerned with beating the opposition. Well, it's true that such quaint notions do hold in the gentler climes of league cricket. In those highly structured forms of the game, everything is subsumed to the vital task of winning the South Eastern Counties

Auto Brake Linings League (Div. 3 South), as of course it should be.

Here at the coalface, in the white heat of so-called friendly matches, the issues are necessarily more complex. Even if the teams hate the sight of each other, the needle thus generated is as nothing compared to the vast baroque networks of needle that already exist within each team. Obviously you need the opposition, and they need you, which is why everyone goes to the considerable effort of cheating each other at every turn. Anything less would imply a lack of respect. But it is within your own team that the competition will be fiercest. Without anything incidental like trophies or prestige to aim at, most 'friendly' sides have long since opted for internal strife. Everyone wants to bat and bowl for as long as possible, and field at cover point. No one wants to umpire or score. Batsmen prefer to play against the easier bowlers, and will try to manipulate the strike so that their partner faces the 6ft 8in West Indian at the other end. If they hit the ball, they will be looking for 2 before their partner has finished his first. If their partner hits the ball, they will saunter through their first run, thus preventing the partner coming back for his second and so stealing the strike. All batsmen wish to bat at number 5 in the order. All bowlers wish to bowl first change, and then come back at the end, when one of the batsmen is eight years old and the other lost a leg at Ypres.

For a long time I thought only Captain Scott was like this. When we began, we wanted a team in which selection played no part. Anyone who wanted to play could play, as long as he booked a place early enough. Players would essentially select themselves. In the end, the people who liked playing the most would play the most often, and everyone would be happy. We were also perfectly willing to accommodate misfits, because we recognised that other people, besides ourselves, might find it hard to settle in teams where their individual talents were not fully appreciated. Now, as our reward, we have a team full of misfits: strong-willed, loud-mouthed psychopaths whose only notion of a team game is one in which they get to do everything they want to and everyone else just makes up the numbers. These are people who cannot find it within their capabilities to bend down and field a ball cleanly – unless they're bowling, in which case they leap around like leopards. Everyone pretends to be dedicated and motivated, and playing for the team, while all the time they are manoeuvring, manipulating, whingeing, wheedling, undermining, bitching, mocking, politicking and, if all else fails, threatening physically, although you need Tim, the perennially angry fast bowler, to be involved if you want genuine bloodshed.

I really did think we were the only team like this. I was amazed that other sides would play us. One or two did actually refuse to after certain embarrassing incidents, but most did not seem to notice. Even if they did, they were more amused than anything else. Then one day I injured myself while dropping a catch (fill in normal excuses here) and had to sit out the rest of the afternoon in the company of the home team. It was an enlightening experience. They sat outside the pavilion, just as we do, in a mumbling threatening pack, exchanging banter and providing their own expert analyses on the state of the game. But also like us, they seemed only peripherally interested in the performances of the opposition. To them we were mere bystanders. If one of our players performed pitifully, they scarcely noticed. But if one of theirs made a mistake, they all went bananas. In fact, the bitching never stopped. Anyone foolish enough to be representing the team out on the field, whether batting or umpiring, was verbally ripped apart. Even if a player did well, the praise was never more than grudging. Yet as soon as the unwitting victim of their invective returned, he was greeted with genuine friendship. He then joined in the excoriation of his absent fellows along with everyone else. Hmm, I thought, perhaps we aren't the only team like this. Further informal investigations have revealed that every team in the country is like this, and very possibly every team in the world.

The problem is that, despite appearances, cricket is not a team game. It is a game for highly motivated individuals who recognise that, for a match to take place, other people have to be present at the same time. Spectators in their infinite innocence presume that, as a team, we are bound together by mutual loyalty and respect, as opposed to the distrust – and, in some cases, hatred – that really has kept our side going all these years. In most team games you genuinely have to operate as a team, supporting each other, helping each other, blending together to create a whole that is infinitely more formidable than the sum of its parts. A cricket team, however, is rarely more than the sum of its parts. Usually it's far less. All those individuals compete feverishly for the best batting position, the most overs, the overall right to do anything they want to – and it's only after these little power struggles have been resolved that anyone turns his attention to the opposition. In our team these little power struggles have never even come close to being resolved.

I suppose we can blame the game itself. You need a strong character to survive in a cricket team. The difference between success and failure can be microscopic. All sports reward success, but few punish failure as cruelly as cricket. One tiny lapse of concentration, and your innings may be over. No one cares that you were batting beautifully, for that huge attempted welly over mid-wicket didn't connect, and that's what everyone will remember. And every bowler knows what it is like to bowl the perfect over – swing, seam, changes of pace, flight, bounce, guile – and see it converted into 18 highly fortunate runs by an oik with a good eye and a 3lb bat. To succeed in cricket takes patience, well-honed skills and a fair portion of luck. To fail in cricket takes about forty-five seconds, including the walk to and from the wicket. The goodhearted get downhearted, leaving the bastards to take up the slack.

Every team is riven by internal disputes of every imaginable kind. A captain might favour one player over another, or worse, favour himself over everyone. Player A may be unable to forgive Player B for running him out in 1982. Grudges harden into full-blooded feuds, until every umpiring decision is so loaded with subtext that the mere question of whether it was out drifts into irrelevance. This is the real meat of village cricket. Spectators don't know what they're missing.

Unfortunately, the old image of village cricket is all but indestructible. It doesn't matter what happens on the field of play. Everyone will still look upon the game as some sort of timeless evocation of an idealised English past. In the mind's eye, lambs will continue to gambol through the buttercups as burly sons of toil dispatch the cherry agriculturally into neighbouring meadows. There's nothing we can do about this. As village cricketers, we have been entrusted with the upkeep of the game's conscience. What a shame, then, that we sold it off in 1985 to buy a couple of pairs of new pads.

CHAPTER FIVE

April

Sheets of torrential rain crash to the ground. Indistinct figures in waterproofs battle through the gales as a swirling river of rainwater washes away small cars, children, anything that hasn't been bolted down against the fearsome winds. You hear your slates peeling away from your roof. The telephone lines are down. There are reports of avalanches in the West Midlands. A huge glacier is said to be about to overwhelm Dorset. Welcome to April.

In the depths of winter, cricket fans pay little attention to the weather. We know it is still out there, doing whatever weather does, but we show no interest. Rain is as nothing to us. Snow is white and fluffy and appealing. None of it matters at all, as we are indoors with the central heating on, watching tapes of old one-day internationals. As long as the fridge is full, we are happy.

But as soon as April arrives, and with it the prospect of a new cricket season (this will be the one, I'll score more runs, take more wickets, won't drop a thing etc. etc.), meteorology suddenly becomes our favourite branch of science. From now until late September, we will check the weather at least a dozen times a day, referring to at least two different newspapers as well as Ceefax and Ian McCaskill on an almost hourly basis. By midsummer we won't even need to read the summaries – we'll just look straight at the isobars. Everything has to be right for the next game. It has to.

April's particular revenge is to foist upon us the most intemperate weather patterns seen this side of Saturn. Men with beards explain this away as a consequence of global warming, but I think the Grim Inevitability of Fate has a hand in it somewhere. April showers we could live with, but we don't get April showers any more. We get April gales interspersed with April snowstorms ('. . . and there's a cold northerly wind sweeping down from the Arctic . . .') and, unforgivably, a two-day April heatwave to destroy our resolve once and for all. It all counts, because as the first weekend of the season grows ever closer, every last hailstorm has a bearing on whether or not the early games will take place. Once again, the strong religious undercurrent in cricket bubbles to the surface. Please, God, please stop this rain. I'll do anything. Please stop it. Please.

But weather-forecasting is an inexact science, dealing in

probabilities rather than certainties, and it relies on the interpretative skills of its practitioners. This is a polite way of saying that you can easily get it wrong, and as all those sad figures who read tealeaves and seaweed routinely demonstrate, with only one screw loose you can be wrong about most things most of the time. As for the Met. Office, their prognostications have been taint.¹ by doubt ever since Michael Fish told us there definitely wouldn't be a hurricane, stop being so silly. For the troubled cricketer, who only wants to know whether he is going to play at the weekend and how many sweaters he should pack, this lack of certainty leaves rather too much room for manoeuvre. Denied the consolation of scientific rigour, he tends to lay his own interpretation over the vaguer prophecies of Messrs Fish, Giles and Kettley. Thus, for cricketing meteorologists, weather-forecasting becomes a matter of temperament rather than measurement. People will see in a weather forecast only what they wish to see, or what they fear to see. Show two cricketers the same forecast, and the chances are that they will interpret it completely differently.

If you're like me, the eternal optimist, you always assume things will clear up. 'Oh don't worry, it'll be fine,' I tell everyone as the tropical thunderstorm rages. The waves are lapping against my bedroom window, but I'm still convinced that the game will go ahead. 'Those Suffolk pitches drain very quickly,' I hear myself assuring people on the phone, even though at the moment you would be unable to reach mid-off without scuba gear.

Harry, by contrast, sees only disaster and misery ahead. For Harry, no weather can ever be clement enough. If the

sun is shining from here to Siberia, he is remembering the
freak downpour at Finchingfield that once washed out a
game in the midst of a heatwave. Should Suzanne Charlton
even hint that there may be a spot of rain around the end of
the week, Harry is out there in his galoshes and sou'wester
battening down the hatches for the expected flood warning.
Animals wander two by two into his West London flat.

And so, on Mondays and Tuesdays, as we are trying to sort
out the teams for the weekend ahead, Harry and I bicker
on the telephone about the long-range weather forecast.
Both of us know that weather can only be forecast to
any degree of accuracy four days into the future. We
know that after that the variables make prediction too
haphazard, and the probabilities are undermined to such
an extent that even the most detailed prediction becomes
little more than a wild guess. We know all this. But while
we both know we are talking nonsense, we both feel
in our livers and kidneys that the following weekend
will witness magnificent Mediterranean sunshine (palm
trees sighted in the Home Counties) or vicious Arctic
squalls (huskies become Britain's best-selling dog). As ever,
rational thought is no match for mindless prejudice. These
ridiculous conversations continue long into the night.

Fortunately, we do have other things to talk about. Whatever the weather, the preparations for a new Captain Scott
season must continue. Fixture lists have been sent out,
Richard has bought some new kit through someone he
knows somewhere who can sort out these things (ask no
questions etc.), most members have paid their annual fees,

and the general air of anticipation is almost edible. To take advantage of this brief interval of good cheer, Harry and I arrange a pre-season jolly in which members can chat, have a few drinks and enjoy each other's company in the sort of relaxed atmosphere that the start of the season proper will render impossible. Just as memories of last season's personal failures have been numbed by five months' intellectual hibernation, so have the collected grudges and arguments that form the backbone of a summer's cricket. Experience has shown that it takes a few weeks of a new season for bitter personal hatreds to flare up into fully fledged international incidents, so any last fragments of goodwill have to be lovingly nurtured while they survive. Like mayflies, however, their life expectancy is brief.

One disadvantage we immediately encounter is the relative shortage of funds. First-class counties can arrange relaxing tours to Portugal and the Bahamas for their young charges, allowing them to ease gently into the pressures of another hectic season. We go to a wine bar off Leicester Square, and ease gently into about fifteen bottles of red wine. Initially, everyone seems delighted to see each other. Backs are slapped, and as the wine is consumed, drunken sentimentality softens people's harder edges. It is wonderful to see them all in such high spirits. Six months ago, several of these players swore they would never speak to each other again. Fingers were prodded in chests. Now all thoughts of vengeance have been abandoned. The slate is clean. X's black eye has long since healed, and Y has nearly forgotten that Z reported him anonymously to the Inland Revenue. The new season is the only season that counts.

The evening meanders along, and the wine continues to flow. The humorous stories about last season's exploits begin, concentrating on those foolish individuals who have neglected to turn up. Poor saps! They should have known better. You don't want to be out of the room when this lot start. Occasional satirical gibes about hairlines and waistlines are made, but all in a spirit of the most generous bonhomie. For God's sake, these are the people with whom you've got to spend every weekend for the next five months. (Another three bottles of house claret? Can I pay by credit card?) Bloody hell, if you can't get on with them for a single evening in a wine bar, you've got no bloody chance. Whoops, sorry, got to go to the loo again.

By 10.30, the mood has subtly altered. Jokes about other players are becoming more pointed, and a fire lights up in the eyes of Tim, our perennially angry fast bowler. This is the time to leave. I am just walking out of the door when I hear the first barbed comment about the notorious run out at Bradenham. The alcove falls silent. One or two other people whisper something about getting their coats. Someone else orders some mineral water. But it is too late. There is no stopping it now. The accusations fly, and all those half-forgotten antipathies burst excitingly to life. Harry's captaincy is torn apart. Before I am five yards down the road, mine will be as well. Selfish batsmanship, lazy fielding, incompetent wicketkeeping, vengeful umpiring, greedy bowling – these are the stuff of conversation now. The cricket season has begun.

*   *   *

It is now just a couple of weeks before the first game, and, having recovered from their hangovers, many Captain Scott players are beginning to toy with the notion of getting fit. It is a moot point, much discussed with friends, wives, girlfriends and other sceptics, just how fit you need to be to play cricket, but it is probably fair to say that you need to be a good deal fitter than we are at this stage. Most of the time I regard my body with a combination of shame and resigned amusement, but in April I almost feel sorry for it. It really has no idea what is in store for it. For months it has led a sheltered life, mollycoddled in the warmth of my flat. But fairly soon it will be called upon to bend down and retrieve passing cricket balls at speed. It will have to run 22 yards at full throttle, spin round, run halfway back down the pitch before the other batsman finally calls 'No!' and scramble back to avoid being run out. It won't enjoy it. It won't, frankly, be up to it. Something has to be done.

Across the country, thousands of cricketers are saying the same thing. Many of us claim to keep fit through the winter, in readiness for the intense physical pressures of the summer weekend grind. It's a wonderful image, isn't it – flabby, out-of-condition non-sportsmen setting out for the gym every winter's morning carrying their kitbags – and I only wish I could believe a word of it. Some of our regulars claim to play five-a-side football every week. It's just that every week the game is unavoidably cancelled, or they are injured, or it was changed to Wednesday and they couldn't do that night. Howard McMinn, our dashing number 3 batsman, used to talk a lot about Rugby Union, and by means of some masterly obfuscation quietly created the impression that he played it every weekend. Well, he certainly watched it every weekend. On Sundays on BBC2. I'd be surprised if he managed anything more energetic during the winter than the odd game of darts.

So in April we panic. Some players institute rigorous keep-fit schemes, and quietly abandon them a few days later. 'Life's too short,' explained one last year, 'and it'll be even shorter if I keep doing fifty press-ups every morning.' One year, in the midst of this early-season mania, I went out for a three-mile run. I won't make that mistake again. By the end I was limping along like a nonagenarian. Children pointed at me and laughed. Sprightly seventy-five-year-olds raced past me. A huge juggernaut splashed me on the Muswell Hill Road and I didn't care. Minutes later, clearly hallucinating, I thought I saw the body of another, less fortunate runner in the adjacent undergrowth. I did what any sensible person would do in the circumstances. I took a cab home.

So instead of getting fit, we arrange some nets. For ten years we have booked weekly April nets at the MCC Indoor School at Lord's, where we limber up, bowl a few full tosses, do Robin Smith eye exercises between balls, and generally convince ourselves that we too could have the reactions of leopards if only we had the time and the inclination. Afterwards we go to the bar, drink lager and eat innumerable packets of crisps. Microwaved pie? Yes, good idea. And perhaps a large vodka for the road.

Sometimes we wonder whether we may have missed the point. In all the other nets, lean young club cricketers prac-tise assiduously. Bowlers run in with purpose, attempting to rediscover line and length and establish a rhythm after months of cold neglect. Batsmen grit it out, playing themselves in, testing their concentration, adjusting technique. In our net batsmen are too busy trying to decapitate their team-mates to bother with technique, grit or concentration. Bowlers don't try to rediscover line and length because they have never found them in the first place. Ten years of nets at Lord's, and we still look far worse than all the other teams there. We're less skilful, substantially fatter and, if Tim is there, more bad-tempered than any other team. Oh, come on! This pitch is too fucking slow! Haven't we got any better balls? Oh, for fuck's sake! The whitewashed brick walls of the Indoor School echo with his random expletives.

Practising in these intimidating surroundings, you are quickly forced to confront your limitations as a cricketer. For all these months you have been drifting in a luscious wintry daze, scoring centuries with ruler and umbrella alike against some of the world's most deadly attacks. You have forgotten that there were excellent reasons for your averaging 2.7 (with the bat) and 83.6 (with the ball) last season. All you can remember is that gloriously timed late cut at Charlton-on-Otmoor, off which you very nearly scored a run.

Nets change all this. My own confidence begins to waver as soon as I walk into the Indoor School and hear the *plock*! of expensive bat on ragged ball. These are the sort of people who cannot help but time their forward defensives. 'Sorry, I tried to kill that one dead, but it just rolled off the sweet spot for 4. Awfully sorry.' Quick drink to steady the nerves, then downstairs to change, and the

first grim whiff of that curious odour of sweaty underwear,
Ralgex and verrucas that characterises the well-patronised
changing room. A few deep breaths, a mild coughing fit,
and out to join my team-mates, who are trying to look as
though they remember which end of the bat to hold. All
internecine rivalries have been suspended for the duration
of the net. We are in this one together. But during these
crucial minutes, as we watch the real cricketers in other
nets, all the disasters of last summer lurch back into our
minds. All the grisly batting failures and run-outs and all
those long hops we bowled in the last over when the other
team only needed 4 to win. Misfields – ugh! Through the
fingers every time. (We would grimace and blow at our
wounded fingers to show how we too were suffering from
the consequences of that misfield, but no one ever seemed
much interested.) All those skiers we dropped. Half an hour
ago we had forgotten all about those skiers. Now we can
remember the precise shapes of the cloud formations as
the ball looped through the air. We remember the silence.
There is no silence in the world like the silence before you
drop a catch. The wind has ceased. Traffic noises have
disappeared. Birds have stopped tweeting. Indeed, every
bird within fifteen square miles has settled on a branch on
the nearest tree to watch you drop this catch. Your hands
are in the air. Your tongue lollops out of your mouth.
The silence is now pregnant, possibly with twins. The ball
completes its upward trajectory. Now it's on its way down.
Vultures are circling. There's no escape now. Ball. Hands.
Fumble. Blast.

   The fantasy world we have patiently created for ourselves

cannot survive such a devastating incursion of reality. Cricket is a game of confidence, and I suspect the only surefire way to maintain that confidence is never to play it. But standing at the business end of the net, gloved, padded, holding this unfamiliar instrument in your hand, you are made nakedly aware of the real depths of your mediocrity. The first ball anyone bowls to me in the first net of the season will be on a perfect length, as straight as Charlton Heston, swinging a touch in the humid atmosphere, slightly too fast for me, and destined to clatter into the middle stump two-thirds of the way down.

Now, and too late, I remember why I don't usually come to nets. What was that we were saying a month ago? 'If Alec Stewart can do it, why can't I?' I wouldn't mind batting as well as Devon Malcolm, let alone the dreaded Stewie. Cricket played in the mind has a pure quality of its own, never allowing itself to be compromised by inconvenient truth. Nets, however, are ruthlessly candid. They conceal nothing from you. By the end of the evening I have been bowled ten times and notionally caught in the slips a further three or four times. I am not moving my feet; I am not thinking fast enough. My reactions are shot to hell. Even if I'm not the best player in the world, or even amongst the top 10 million, I always felt that I knew the basics. But at the first net of the season, you don't know the basics any more. You have to relearn what you have learned a hundred times before. You effectively have to start from scratch.

That evening, in the depth of gloom, I drink too much and wonder whether I should take up backgammon instead.

The following morning, a vast new aggregation of chickens comes home to roost. This was, after all, my first serious exercise since my attempts to murder Arvind on last year's end-of-season tour. Accordingly, when I awake, rigor mortis appears to have set in. My muscles are all screaming at me, some in language I didn't know they knew. Perhaps it is time to buy one of those electrical stairlifts they advertise on Channel 4. A Radox bath seems the only short-term solution, although with that there's always the risk that once I'm in, I may never be able to get out.

What we get from a net, therefore, is not useful practice, for as will become clear, nets have no bearing on the cricket any of us will eventually play. What we get from a net is a profound sense of our innate inferiority, a chronic hangover and an inability to walk without assistance for three days. It is intriguing to think that we are supposed to do all this for fun.

The first match looms, and you are still going to nets. By net three, you are occasionally getting to the pitch of the ball. By net four, your bowling is passable. You are beginning to enjoy yourself. MCC has played the champion county; the match has ended in a draw. Leicestershire are playing Oxford University at The Parks. Leicestershire declared on 515 for 2. Oxford are 17 for 8 in reply. You have caught your first sight of Tony Lewis on the television. His eyebrows are even bushier than they were last year. What do they do with Tony Lewis in the winter? You trust he is well looked after. The season is gearing up. After half a dozen nets, and a little patient coaching from a kind colleague, your confidence has slowly improved. Perhaps you're not so bad after all. Perhaps this will be the season.

And then you go out and play a proper game and remember again why you don't usually come to nets. For four or five weeks you have been playing in regulated conditions: indoors, in the warmth, on a reliable, entirely predictable surface. Controlled temperatures have allowed bowlers to warm up gradually. Batsmen have grown used to the regular bounce and the way the ball comes sweetly on to the bat.

It is laughable to think that this is supposed to prepare you in some way for the first game of the season, which is played in a howling gale on a typical April pudding with optional cowpats. Bowlers bowl as they have done in the nets and tear twenty-three muscles. No cricket for them until July. For batsmen, the ball is suddenly behaving in ways that nets could never begin to help you predict. The bowler bowls, the ball pitches, and about three days later it arrives at your bat, long after you've played the shot, trudged back to the pavilion, had a shower and gone home. Pride may come before a fall, but nets come before a nought.

And each year, so lulled are we into a warm, indoor, utterly fallacious sense of security that it all comes as a surprise. We stride out to the crease oozing confidence, and wander back a minute or two later utterly dejected. Never, in sixteen years of Scott service, have I begun the season with anything other than a 0. Sometimes they have been long, attritional 0s, full of character and spunk. Mostly they have been brief, risible 0s, with me playing far too early and the ball bobbling hopelessly up to short mid-off.

The simple explanation is that it is still winter. All those nets prepare you for summer, but although cricket is historically 'the summer game', the season begins long before anything remotely resembling summer has arrived. Every April, when the early-season tourists arrive, the ones who have never toured here before cannot believe how cold it is, or that anyone would want to play cricket in such weather. Nor can we – and we have been playing here all our lives.

Back in 1985 our first game of the season was against Sidney Sussex College, Cambridge – a plum fixture for us, because we were used to playing Oxford second teams and Cambridge colleges are generally too snobby to have second teams. This was the full might of the First XI, rangy, firm-jawed bastards one and all. Our best hope was for a draw, and we got it, but not in the way we expected. For this was April, and an unusually cold and forbidding April at that. We lost the toss and fielded first, and our fast-bowling ringer took a couple of wickets before the home side's blatant superiority began to tell. But it was getting colder and colder, and after an hour it started to snow. We were so cold that for a couple of minutes we just stood there, unable to move. Not that all of us wanted to leave the field. Bob Jones, our well-upholstered leg-spinner, wanted to stay on to see if the ball would turn off the snow. But by this time the outfield had changed colour, so we shuffled gratefully towards the pavilion. A log fire blazed invitingly within. We took an early tea, just in case the snow stopped. By 4.30 three inches of snow had settled on a good length. Only then, as body temperatures returned to normal, did

Neal, who had been standing in as wicketkeeper, realise that two of his fingers were broken.

A more consistently Arctic fixture has been Marsh Gibbon in Buckinghamshire, the only known tundra wicket in the south-east of England. The pitch sits on a lofty and isolated plateau, vulnerable to every meteorological whim. Polar bears wander freely in the surrounding fields. Captain Scott players never go anywhere unprepared, and one particularly chilly fielding session saw a spontaneous outbreak of woolly scarves, at least one overcoat and, from Terence at deep third man, a balaclava. By the time a bowler had put on all his layers after finishing an over, it was time to take them off again for his next over. Only my friend Stephen had come unprepared, but with admirable resourcefulness he found a dirty old blue plastic bin-liner which, after tearing the end open, he put on over his head. It looked like a prototype for an all-over body condom. He couldn't move his arms, but then he wasn't exactly the most skilled fielder on the side anyway, so it didn't reduce his effectiveness by much. At least he fell on top of the ball a couple of times.

These days we kick off at Englefield Green in Surrey, another beautiful venue so open to the elements that even when it's sunny, you are a fool not to wear at least three sweaters and a full set of thermals. Here, it would seem, is the perfect opportunity for us to emulate the high standards set by our mentor, the Captain. Not for nothing do we wear caps inscribed with our team motto '*Modo Egredior*' ('I am just going outside'). But the wetness of the thirtysomething middle-class English male is deeply entrenched. For each year, in the first game of the season, we remember something else we have forgotten during the wasted winter months: that in April the ball is remarkably hard. When it hits your hands, you drop it. Every year at Englefield Green, we drop cartloads. So you have played only one game, your batting has collapsed, your bowling is a pale imitation of itself, and your fielding has gone to pot. Nothing like a good start to the season.

CHAPTER SIX

O My Solkar and My Abid Ali, Long Ago

Only the warm glow of nostalgia can dispel that April chill. Cricket loves its past. It's terrified of the future, and not too sure about the present, but the past it adores.

Just look at the glint in Tony Lewis's eye whenever the umpires come off for bad light. For a few wondrous moments we can forget England's current travails and wallow without guilt in some cosily repackaged view of cricket's glorious past. First we shall see the edited highlights of a 1973 one-day international, or perhaps ancient black-and-white footage of something from the 1960s. Meanwhile, BBC researchers are trawling the bars of Lord's for ancient ex-cricketers who can reminisce on air about the good old days. On they creak, with egg on their ties and no real idea of what day it is, and blather away about Bradman's Australians and what about old Wilfred Rhodes, now there was a real character. This isn't cheap television so much as free television, but it is enthralling nonetheless. Call me sentimental, but there is something oddly consoling about the idea of these old buffers hanging around Test match grounds decades after retirement waiting to be interviewed by Tony Lewis. They may be watery of eye and have knuckles like table-tennis balls, but their long-term memories are unimpaired. Some of them can drone on for days, and often do.

The immense good fortune of cricket's buffer fraternity is that it has so much to reminisce about. Decades of polishing these anecdotes have given them a lustre that more recent cricketing exploits tend to lack. This is a tragedy for those of us who have come to cricket since the invention of the combustion engine. Our own nostalgic baggage, denied the patina of age, is almost depressingly prosaic. How joyous it must be to have been inspired by the authority of Len Hutton or the brio of Gilbert Jessop. How wondrous to recall the energy and aggression of Neil Harvey or the enormous beard of W.G. Grace.

My own first vivid memory of cricket, by contrast, is of Abid Ali destroying England's middle order at Manchester in 1971. It could so easily have been Barry Richards or Clive Lloyd or Dennis Lillee, or even Geoffrey Boycott, who persuaded me that cricket was the game of games. Or perhaps Mike Proctor, or Derek Underwood, or anyone, really, but Abid Ali – or 'S. Abid Ali' as we fans liked to call him. In 1971, India were still famous for their distinctive trio of devilish spin-bowlers, Venkatagharavan, Chandrasekhar and Bishen Bedi, unconscious progenitor of cricket's only amusing pun, 'Bedi byes'. In years to come I would draw unholy pride from my ability to spell Venkatagharavan, and cheer when an unrelated politician called Chandrasekhar was briefly elected Prime Minister of India. At the time, though, I was eleven years old and a Chelsea supporter, and these names meant nothing to me. All I knew, from what Jim Laker had said on BBC1, was that the three spinners were a considerable threat to England, while Abid Ali and Solkar, the lowly medium-pacers who came on at the beginning to take the shine off the ball, were there purely to make up the numbers. In 1971 England had John Snow, the sort of burly fast bowler who could have come out of a mine, had there been any mines in Sussex, and Peter Lever, another of the many England fast bowlers who were never quite as good as you hoped they were going to be. The legendary figure of J.S.E. Price, whose run-up started somewhere in the stands, was also in selectorial favour.

In comparison, Solkar and Abid Ali looked totally harm- less. Short of stature – though, of course, not as small as Little Harry Pilling – they had about them the distinct air of cannon fodder. The commentators were polite, but even an unusually trusting prepubescent like me got the distinct impression that any batsman would be able to see them off as long as he didn't forget to bring his bat out with him.

And yet, over the years, Solkar came to dismiss Geoffrey Boycott so many times that some bold observers were even heard to whisper the word 'bunny' in connection with the great man. And on the morning of 5 August 1971, Abid Ali disposed of Jameson (on his debut), Edrich, Fletcher and D'Oliveira to leave England on 41 for 4.

For most recent England teams, 41 for 4 would be a normal day at the office. We would just be grateful they weren't 41 for 5. Oh, there goes another one. But in 1971 Ray Illingworth's team had played twenty-five successive Tests without defeat. Since losing the First Test to Australia in 1968 (and eventually drawing the series 1–1), they had drawn 0–0 in Pakistan, beaten both West Indies and New Zealand at home 2–0, regained the Ashes 2–0 in Australia, won 1–0 in New Zealand and beaten the emerging Pakistanis 1–0 at home. Just typing out this list gives me a vicarious thrill, all the more pathetically because I never saw any of the games. Chelsea-worship might not have lasted long, but it was long enough for me to miss England's most successful run in cricket history. Then Abid Ali came along and reduced this talented side to 41 for 4.

The difference between then and now is that England came back to score 386. Illingworth himself scored 107 and Peter Lever, batting at number 9, remained unbeaten on 88. India scored 212, Brian Luckhurst scored a century in the second innings and Abid Ali didn't take another wicket for the rest of the series. Had it not bucketed down on the fifth day, England might even have won. Their unbeaten run remained intact, albeit not for long, as Chandrasekhar got them in the final Test at The Oval.

A draw, then, and not a particularly gripping one. And

yet this Test made the profoundest impression upon me. Soon I was immune to the blandishments of Osgood, Bonetti and 'Chopper' Harris. Cricket took me for its own. Clearly something about the score 41 for 4 had awoken a nascent urge within my puny frame. For on that first morning, as Abid Ali bowled his little wobblies and England collapsed in abject submission, I developed a nose for cricketing failure and mediocrity that has stayed with me ever since.

Everyone remembers the successes. Look at Ian Botham's huge beaming face on *A Question of Sport*. No one could hope to dent the carapace of his giant self-regard. He knows that we all love him, despite his flaws and his madnesses, or even because of them. In 1981, as no one will ever forget, Botham played two remarkable innings against Kim Hughes' Australians and almost single-handedly turned the series. If ever a phrase were associated with a cricketer, 'almost single-handedly' is associated with Ian Botham. At Headingley, he put on 100-odd with Graham Dilley, another 50-odd with Chris Old and a vital handful with Bob Willis before being beached on 149 not out. When your girlfriend has abandoned you for a quantity surveyor or you have been out first ball for the fourth match in succession, this is the video you go home and watch over and over again, long into the night.

Four weeks later, at Old Trafford, Botham scored 118, an innings born not of desperation, as at Headingley, but of absolute self-belief. It was one of the most clinically destructive batting displays most of us had ever seen. But who was at the other end? Who was sharing this great day? Whoever it was can't have been scoring many runs, otherwise we would all remember him. This of course is the great clue. By a process of elimination we can deduce that only one batsman could possibly have shared in this magnificent moment. Only one man could have effaced himself so totally as to be forgotten by an entire generation of cricket-lovers. Step forward Chris Tavaré, hero of this hour.

In the first innings England had scored 231, assisted by a last-wicket stand of 56 from Allott and Willis. Australia crumbled to 130 (M.F. Kent 52, Willis 4–63, Botham 3–28). But by the time Botham came in on Saturday afternoon, England had squandered their advantage in their usual spineless fashion. After 69 overs of their second innings, they had amassed only 104 for 5 on a pitch that was growing steadily easier. Surely Australia would not make the same mistake a second time. The initiative was theirs once again. Then Botham arrived and astonished everyone by playing himself in. It took him 53 balls and 70 minutes to reach 28. We wondered whether his drinks had been laced. ('Ah, Mr Botham, an aperitif?') In fact, he was merely waiting for Alderman and Lillee to take the second new ball. With vicious precision, he reached his 100 off only another 33 balls. He hit six 6s, a record for Anglo–Australian Tests. It was breathtaking stuff.

Meanwhile, at the other end, Tavaré twitched and prodded and wandered quietly about. Of the 149 he added with Botham, his share was 28. His 78 eventually took 7 hours. His 306-minute 50 was the slowest half-century in all

English first-class cricket, and the third slowest in Tests. As Botham brought the crowd to its feet, Tavaré did his utmost to make them sit down again. Here was dullness personified, a walking, twitching anaesthetic. With his long face and little moustache, Tavaré was cricketer-as-bank clerk, a batsman apparently devoid of all personality. At the other end was a man larger than life; at Tavaré's end, a man so much smaller than life that electron microscopes might reasonably have been called into action. I knew instinctively that he was just as singular as Botham, and in many ways more interesting.

For Tavaré never disappointed you. Others came in, flashed about, irresponsibly scored a few runs, but Tavaré just stayed there, prodding. After each ball he walked a few feet to square leg, paused, and walked back again. This became compulsive to watch. Every ball: prod, pause, walk, pause, walk, pause, prod. This was cricket for which normal states of consciousness simply did not prepare you. Botham's batting was an affirmation of life. Tavaré's batting was a denial of hope. Life was to be battled through, although to what end remained uncertain. As Tavaré's endless innings proceeded, and bodies fell with increasing regularity from tenth-storey windows, the sheer grinding pointlessness of his unflinching concentration seemed to acquire a significance of its own. There was a stillness at the heart of a Tavaré innings that was almost Nordic in its bleakness. Had Ingmar Bergman been at Old Trafford that day, I feel sure he would have identified Tavaré as a kindred spirit. Geoffrey Boycott is fond of expressing the conviction that if you stay there long enough, runs will automatically come. Not with Tavaré, they didn't. If he stayed there long enough, then at the end of it, he was still there. He was the ultimate existential cricketer.

His finest hour came in Madras in January 1982. There, on a classic subcontinental featherbed, Keith Fletcher told his batsmen to 'bat as long as you like'. We can only imagine the whoops of joy that Tavaré uttered on receiving such an instruction. On second thoughts, perhaps we can't: even in a state of ecstasy, it's hard to envisage Tavaré doing much more than raising a thoughtful eyebrow. And so, with teeth gritted and not a single thought of crashing off-drives or square cuts in his mind, Tavaré walked out with Graham Gooch to open the batting. Gooch, who obviously hadn't been paying attention, passed 50 in an hour on his way to a fluent 127. Tavaré scored 35 in 5 hours and 34 minutes. That's a run every 9 minutes and 32.6 seconds. What cruelty to inflict on the eager Indian public. What joy for his fans back home. My only regret was that I was not there to see it. Trees have grown more quickly than he batted that day.

But we live in a shallow, facile world whose citizens demand endless excitement to enrich their otherwise drab lives. Tavaré's feats of concentration were regarded with contempt by spectators and journalists alike. He became – one dreads to mention it even now – something of a figure of fun. Eventually even the England management tired of his supreme singlemindedness. Tavaré was dropped, and returned to the relative obscurity of county cricket. How casually we waste talent in this country. An average of 33 isn't bad, especially if you are only scoring those runs every 9 minutes and 32.6 seconds. In later years, the England

selectors realised the error of their ways, and tried a handful
of other notable barnacles. C.W.J. Athey was the most
promising, but even he spoiled the effect by occasionally
scoring runs. In the meantime Tavaré poked and prodded
with distinction for Kent and Somerset, latterly as captain
of each.

But Tavaré's story does not end there. For as retirement
loomed, something within his ordered, disciplined mind
flipped. Perhaps the endless defensive manoeuvres had
worn him down. Perhaps he just went mad. But Tavaré's
change of heart was as sudden as it was unexpected.
No longer did he treat every ball like an unexploded
bomb. Forward defensives had lost their appeal. Instead,
a huge scything backlift told the bowler that he meant
business. Loose balls were dispatched with startling ferocity.
Even good-length balls received the full treatment. The
bank clerk had become a bank manager, and run off to
Brazil with the contents of the safe. It wasn't the clown
playing Hamlet – this was a Shakespearean actor wilfully
impersonating Bernard Manning. All our preconceptions
had been turned upside-down. If he had undergone a sex
change I doubt we could have been more surprised.

The big question was: was this the real Tavaré? Had he
been labouring for years under an intolerable burden of
inhibition, desperate to transform, however briefly, from
defensive duck to free-flowing swan? More credible was
the theory that this was a form of mid-life crisis – the
cricketing equivalent of having an affair with your secretary
and wearing a baseball cap back to front to hide your bald
patch. As you would expect, there were no answers from

Tavaré. Even at his most violent, he looked exactly the same. He still trudged to square leg between balls. The little moustache never even quivered.

Perhaps the thought had struck Tavaré that after a so-so Test career, and as a solid performer rather than a charismatic ground-filler, he would forever be regarded as a nearly man. English cricket is jam-packed with nearly men. Heroes, for one reason or another, are in desperately short supply, but of nearly men there is a clear abundance. From schools and colleges nationwide, nearly men emerge in huge numbers, nearly graduating to county cricket or, if they do gain a regular place, nearly nudging those much-nudged selectors should they happen to score a couple of elegant 50s. A handful, after nearly being picked for ages, are finally chosen for England when they are nearly at the end of a bounteous run of form – the precise end coming as they walk out on to the field for a Test match for the first time. Some of these nearly men are never selected again, although they're nearly always mentioned in dispatches when cricket correspondents are assessing likely Test candidates. Others come in and out of the side on a regular basis, and nearly make it, but not quite. Thus there are so many levels of nearliness in cricket that virtually everyone who plays it for a living is a nearly man of some sort. It should be no surprise that, after all these near misses, England so often nearly win. Or nearly draw. Or nearly lose by only a small margin.

I remember virtually nothing about summer holidays from the early seventies, but I do remember sitting outside a bar, somewhere in the Mediterranean, reading on the back page of someone else's *Daily Express* that Frank Hayes had scored a century on his Test debut. I only read a couple of paragraphs before the *Express* reader noticed me and twisted acrobatically around so I could not even read The Gambols. Money was tight at the time, or at least my father was, so I could not buy a newspaper for myself. For the rest of the holiday I thought of little but this century. A new batting star had arrived. Praise the Lord! Out with the flags and bunting! Perhaps they would stop picking Keith Fletcher at last. The few newspapers I later managed to get hold of predicted great things for Hayes. But the Curse of the Nearly Men claimed him almost immediately. In his 8 subsequent Tests, he never scored more than 29.

I am not sure that English cricket has ever recovered. Hayes was destroyed by too much praise and promise. Ever since, both press and public have been careful not to laud English cricketers in any circumstances whatsoever. It wouldn't do for them to get too big-headed. But the Curse of the Nearly Men was never lifted. Few burn out quite like Hayes. More typical are the Boomerang Club, those select players who pop in and out of the England team as regularly and nonchalantly as the rest of us go to the shops. For years I was gripped by the career of Graham Roope, who had that helpful habit (recently emulated by C.C. Lewis) of doing well against poor teams and fouling up consistently against the good ones. And yet, despite averaging only 30, and never scoring more than 77, he was picked again and again. Even as a twelve-year-old I remember being massively frustrated by this, as though

the selectors were doing it on purpose. Thus were the
two great cricketing paranoias imprinted early upon my
developing personality.

1: The selectors choose mediocre players on purpose,
   just to annoy you.
2: If you go out of the room while England are batting,
   someone will be out and it will be your fault.

Roope would come in for a couple of Tests, score a few
promising 23s, be left out, and then come back for another
couple of Tests the following summer. Or else he would
go on tour because he was a 'good tourist'. This meant
he could score promising 23s all over the world, a rare
and distinctive talent.

Later on Geoff Miller filled this crucial role. Roo[pe]
played 21 Tests; between 1976 and 1984 Miller managed
remarkable 34. He didn't do altogether badly – he average[d]
25 with the bat and took 60 wickets at 31. But, again like
C.C. Lewis, his greatest talent was for being picked. He
remains famous for three things: a droopy moustache
that was pendulous even by 1970s' standards; for catching
the ball parried by Tavaré (hooray!) which dismissed Jeff
Thomson and gave England that staggering 3-run victory
on the 1982–3 Ashes tour; and for twice scoring 98 in Test
matches. In 1977–8 at Lahore he ran out of partners while
on 98 not out, never having scored a first-class century.
Five years later, he still hadn't scored a first-class century,
but once again reached 98, this time against India, and
was caught at silly point. The moustache drooped so low

you thought it was going to drop off. What was bizarre
was not that he kept missing that elusive century, but
that not having scored a century, he so often batted for
England at number 5. Perhaps he possessed incriminating
photographs of Alec Bedser, or had kidnapped members
of A.C. Smith's family.

Possibly the shortest route to becoming a nearly man is by
nearly taking wickets, which was Mike Hendrick's speciality.
'Ooof!' 'Aaargh!' and 'Eeee!' were but three of the cries
regularly expelled from spectators' mouths as he passed the
outside edge yet again. He was, we were told, 'the unluckiest
bowler in cricket'. Batsmen played and missed, then played
and missed again. Hunched and impassive, weighed down
by the unfairness of it all, Hendrick trudged back to his
mark and started again. English fastish bowlers fall into
two well-defined groups – the aggressive ones (Botham,
Gough) and the gloomy exhausted ones. Hendrick was
about as gloomy and exhausted as a bowler can get
without passing out. His heir is Angus Fraser, who bowls
frightening numbers of overs a year and yet, after a single
ball of a Test match, looks tired, flushed, bored, furious
and resigned, even if he has just bowled someone middle
stump. Hendrick had this approach off pat. Once he even
grew a gloomy beard, presumably in a last-ditch attempt to
depress the batsman into nicking the ball. But the batsman
never did nick the ball. So Hendrick trudged back to his
mark and started again. In the end he took 87 Test wickets
at 25.83, so he must have been doing something right. It
just didn't feel like it at the time.

*   *   *

If ever I had a real hero, it was that most frustratingly gifted of nearly men, Derek Randall. When Graham Gooch and Geoffrey Boycott organised their tour of thick-witted mercenaries to South Africa in 1982, they accidentally did England cricket a great favour. Randall had been out of the side since the 1979–80 tour of Australia, when someone had decided to turn him into an opening batsman. I had always wondered about this, as Brearley's side already had three opening batsmen, and Randall was clearly not suited to the task. But he was such an amiable character that he went along with this crazy plan, and ended up scoring 26 runs in the Tests at an average of 6.5.

Only when the dimwits took the South African Breweries' shilling was Randall again considered. He played regularly for the next two years under Bob Willis's and later David Gower's leadership. For me Randall represented the extremes of cricketing fortune. When he was good he was as good as anyone could ever be. His stroke play had a glorious effrontery that all the usual Randall adjectives ('impish', 'mischievous') could not begin to convey. And when he was bad he was dreadful, a lost soul. Sometimes, as when he scored 100 opening against Imran Khan's Pakistanis in 1982, he overcame poor form with pure determination. But, like David Gower, he seemed to encapsulate the fragility of even the most talented batsman's existence. In virtually every innings of his you could be sure to see flashes of genius and quite startling incompetence, often in the same over.

He performed best when put at number 6 or 7, where he averaged 47. If only his respective captains had stopped trying to turn him into an opener, or even a number 3. They should have realised that with Ian Botham in the side, Randall was England's luxury. Other lesser players – Allan Lamb is one who particularly springs to mind – had their every whim accommodated. Randall was always the one who was about to be dropped, even when he had done well. After that First Test of 1984, when once again he had been needlessly sacrificed at number 3, he never played for England again.

The innings I remember most fondly came in the Fourth Test against New Zealand in 1983, when England, as usual, were faltering on 169 for 5. Botham scored one of his more ebullient 100s at the other end, and took most of the credit, but it was the way Randall laid into his county colleague, His Serene Highness Sir Richard Hadlee, that really made you sit up and pay attention. In one over he scored 20 off him, and Hadlee didn't bowl a bad ball. Each one was pitched on a good length just outside off-stump, and five out of six were stroked effortlessly through the off-side for 4. Each shot was subtly different but faultlessly executed. It was precision batting, inch-perfect and uncompromisingly aggressive. He scored 83, and the partnership of 186 in 32 overs won the match.

It was Randall's bad luck that he enjoyed his best season in 1985, when England's batsmen were destroying Allan Border's Australians. You felt he never quite fitted in with the prevailing clique, which is why, although he played 47 Tests, he never achieved what he might have done. Nearly, nearly, nearly.

*   *   *

Ah, all this nostalgia is almost too exhilarating. The problem is that time erodes even the most vivid of cricketing memories. Eventually all you are left with is a series of random snapshots, which bear little relation to the way things were, but which have to do. Bev Congdon, the New Zealand batsman of the early seventies, now appears in my memory as little more than an extended chin. I remember that he was 'obdurate', and I remember the chin – no more. Colin Dredge of Somerset, a bowler more gloomy and exhausted than even the great Hendrick. Alan Hill of Derbyshire, an amazingly pedestrian batsman who somehow managed to retain his county place for fifteen years. Rodney Marsh shouting a lot. Jeff Thomson's calamitous peroxide experiment on the 1985 Ashes tour. Ian Botham's even more disastrous barnet thereafter. Ray East of Essex, a 'joker'. Were you laughing? Me neither. The magisterial Pringle, selected many thousands of times for England, graduating from promising young shaver to wily old pro without the usual phase of being good somewhere in the middle. The One-Test Club of the late seventies and eighties: Alan Butcher (v. India, 1979), Paul Parker (v. Australia, 1981), Mark Benson (v. India, 1986). What did they do wrong? Gus Logie, who never did anything very much against any other country but always came good when the West Indies were 80 for 4 against England, whereupon England would collapse in the second innings and lose the series 5–0. The one Test David Gower captained in 1982 against Pakistan when Bob Willis was injured, and it seemed as though England had selected the feeblest bowling attack in Test history: Botham (out of sorts), Robin Jackman (a trouper in the event), Pringle, Hemmings, Ian Greig. I don't even have to look that one up to check it: it is seared on my memory. (Pakistan won by 10 wickets.) Boycott's hundredth 100 against Australia in 1977. The tears flowed. Majid Khan's odd-coloured pads on his last tour of England in 1982. Zaheer Abbas, fearsomely talented, with a grave tendency to score large 200s against England. I just wish I had been grown up enough at the time to enjoy his batting for its own sake, rather than wanting him to be out every ball. Jim Laker called him 'studious' because he wore glasses. Peter Willey, with his small boy's face and forearms like hams. I always presumed that his rugged beardy macho image was an unconscious reaction to his youthful looks. Certainly he appeared to be able to go months without blinking. More blubs when he scored that excellent gritty 100 against the West Indies in 1980, putting on 116 for the last wicket with Bob Willis to save the match. David Steele, the first of Northamptonshire's many England batsmen: 50 and 45 in 1975 on his debut at Lord's, against Lillee and Thomson in full flight. Ross Edwards being dismissed for 99 in the same match, lbw to a Woolmer full toss. Oh, the joy. Another huge antipodean chin: any relation to Bev? C.L. Smith, out lbw to Hadlee on his first ball in Test cricket. Tony Greig saying on *Nationwide* that he would make the West Indies grovel. The feelings of hurt and betrayal when Greig turned out to be at the centre of the Packer coup. Edrich and Close taking 77 minutes to move from 1 to 2 against the West Indies at Old Trafford in 1976. Sandeep Patil scoring 129 not out against England in 1982 and then going off to become a film star. Ian

Botham going to Hollywood to become a film star, and
then coming back. Trevor Chappell, doomed not to be as
good as Ian or Greg. Really, really *hating* Greg Chappell.
The dread fear of Abdul Qadir before he first set foot in
the UK. Ditto Mushtaq Ahmed. Ditto Shane Warne, with
knobs on. Terry Alderman's curious resemblance to a chap
I knew at university. Wondering in 1976 and 1980 whether
Viv Richards would *ever* be out . . .

CHAPTER SEVEN

May

The routine has begun: cricket on Saturdays, cricket on Sundays, aching limbs and Weltschmerz on Monday mornings. May is a wonderful month for Scott fixtures. There are several trips to villages we have been playing for years and know well, and our Oxford origins are represented by a handful of games against college second teams, on beautiful well-tended pitches in sometimes magnificent surroundings, with the added attraction, if luck is truly favouring us, of an all-day bar in the pavilion. At this stage I am possessed of such rabid enthusiasm that I put myself down for every game. This is a quick and easy way of using up all your stocks of rabid enthusiasm before the season has barely started. But only a fool would resist the

Rain Men

prospect of easy runs in those Oxford fixtures. It's odd how the prospect of easy runs never quite translates to real live easy runs: the students can never resist importing a hotshot bowler from the First XI ('University side next year, so they say'), who slices through our batting order like a machete through butter. But it's the prospect that counts. At first glance the village oppositions are more formidable, but at this time of year they tend to be hampered by the parallel concerns of the local football team, which may either have embarked on a heroic cup run, or be engaged in a plucky and almost certainly doomed attempt to avoid relegation. This has the effect of decanting all the available talent from their cricket team, which usually leaves them with a load of old crocks to match our fit and agile squad of marginally younger crocks. Add the constant threat of rain, which customarily decimates the early-season fixture list, and you are presented with half a dozen watertight reasons to put yourself down for every match going. So I do, and stumble through every Monday in a haze of exhaustion and numb irritability. Tuesday, too, if by some miracle I scored some of those 'easy' runs.

At one of these early games, some idiot will say that what we really need is a three-day weekend. Never time to do anything, always a rush at Tesco, my girlfriend is barely speaking to me, blah, blah, blah. He's wrong, of course. If we did have an extra day, someone would arrange a fixture for it.

So it's up at the crack of 9.30 on Sunday morning, with that strange sensation that overnight your brain has been surgically removed and replaced by a gigantic blob of ear wax. Tragically, the game you look forward to most is inevitably preceded by a night of intense revelry, which is why it now feels as though your tongue has been recarpeted and a microscopic road crew is building a bypass through your temporal lobes. Back in the old single days, when sitting around in pubs wondering why we didn't have girlfriends was *de rigueur*, an entirely hungover team was commonplace. But that was a while ago. Now most people in the team have wives, children, sensible cars and that indefinable air of defeat that adult life brings. Unfortunately, the responsibilities of adulthood have done little to soften their tempers. By eleven o'clock I have already fielded half a dozen impatient phone calls from members keen to confirm that the game is still on. This presents problems, because I don't know myself whether or not the game is on. Indeed, I have been trying all morning to get through to Harry, who in turn is trying to get through to the representative of the home team, who is either out looking at the pitch to assess whether it's still playable, or back home trying to call Harry. The engaged signal is as central to a day's cricket as pads, balls and stones in the umpire's coat. You can easily spend half an hour on the telephone without ever getting through to anybody. Sometimes you call someone who isn't even playing because you need to prove to yourself that not everyone you know is frantically trying to ring everyone else.

Eventually, the good news filters through. There was a little light rain over the Cotswolds late last night, but at Chuffington Magna the sun is now breaking through the clouds. According to the Met. Office, there is a 20 per cent probability of a shower this afternoon; otherwise the forecast is good. The game is on.

All necessary calls are made, except to Martin Dyckhoff, our ex-fast bowler, who lives miles away and has already set off. Five minutes after I have left, he will finally get through to my answering machine from a phone box in a motorway service station. I pack my kit, including a book (which I shan't read), two pens (both of which I shall lose), a T-shirt to wear under my shirt if it's cold, two sweaters if it's very cold, my own private box, a spare pair of trousers and even one or two things I might need. I am getting a lift from Terence, who lives a couple of miles from me in North London. Terence has been giving me lifts to cricket matches for sixteen years. I don't think he minds this, even though the laws of banter-based friendship demand that he complains incessantly. Again, this shows how much our lives have changed since we started the team. A dozen years ago, lifts were a savage bone of contention. Sometimes people talked of little else. At university, or in the early years of London poverty, cars were a rarity. To give someone a lift was therefore to grant a huge and unreturnable favour, akin to lending him a substantial sum of money, or saving his brother's life. You had to be careful whom you asked for a lift. Some drivers would charge a mere pound for petrol, but one notorious tightwad asked far more, and still only dropped you on the slip road of the M40. One player, who had two minutes to catch his last train, was dropped ten minutes' walk from Paddington Station, but was too astonished to say anything. He just sloped off, dazed. He didn't last long. These days most players drive everywhere, and are so bored by it that they are quite happy to give lifts, if only for the company.

Chuffington Magna CC, our pseudonymous opponents for today, are an amiable load of wasters who serve an excellent tea. On the way up Terence and I discuss who is playing. It's Sunday and I am captaining, so I sketch out a putative batting order in my little black book. My little black book accompanies me everywhere. Within its sturdy black binding, elegantly embossed with the legend 'Rymans', it stores the definitive team lists for every game, and also acts as my cricketing memo pad. Whenever a player books in a game, it is recorded here. A needlessly elaborate system of ticks and crosses indicates whether or not the player who booked is a club member, whether he has confirmed and so forth. Everyone who runs a cricket team has a book like this, the loss of which he fears more than death itself. The book also records for generations as yet unborn how many games everyone has played for us, both this season and over the club's sixteen-year history. This has bearings on club membership, for to become a member, and stay a member, you need to play a certain number of games a season. Membership allows you to play any game you like, as long as you book a week ahead and eleven other members haven't sneaked in before you. For this they pay £25 at 1994 prices: we charge no match fee. Originally we instituted this system to save ourselves effort. Only later did we discover that people love being members of things, whether or not they take advantage of their status. At the moment we have twenty-two members, of whom a third struggle to play half a dozen games a year. Non-members have to play far more to get in, and must rely on existing members not wanting to play. Only the truly enthusiastic get in, which is as it should be.

The little black book records it all. How I love and cherish the statistics that reside within its pages. Some cricketers pretend that they have no time for statistics. They are liars. No cricketer has lived who does not know his career batting average, even if it is only a hopelessly rough guess to two decimal places. In my little black book I record the appearances partly because I need to for important administrative reasons, but mainly because I want to for sad anally retentive reasons. Harry, who is more interested in the way people play than the fact of their playing, maintains the batting and bowling averages. He thinks such things are important. Admittedly, he does appear in the top half of both averages, while I don't bowl and have a lifetime batting average of 4.2. Well, since you ask, 4.1956, top score 35. My particular skill is more specialised. I turn up. So far I have turned up to 252 games for Captain Scott. I may not have achieved much in those games, but at least I was there.

Even on appearances, though, Harry beats me. There is a very good reason for his having scored more runs and taken more wickets than anyone else: he has played far more games. Not to put too fine a point on it, he has played in them all. Up to the end of the 1994 season, we had played 393 games, of which Harry had played 393. Such singlemindedness is rare, certainly outside the realms of psychological textbooks. The scale of his achievement has boggled some of Europe's finest minds. Harry likes to belittle it. So what if he has played all the games? There just wasn't one he didn't want to play. On a disingenuousness scale, this seems to me fairly close to 'I was only following orders', but you can't fault his dedication. In truth he has overcome apparently insurmountable obstacles to acquire this record, not all of them placed there by his team-mates. His wife, as if primed by the fixture list, was considerate enough to go into labour on a Monday and give birth early on Wednesday morning, allowing Harry to play both games the following weekend. A few years ago, when we were playing at Stansfield in Suffolk, Harry's car broke down in Tooting. He rang up Cliff, our run-out expert, for a lift, and they arranged to meet outside a distant North London tube station. Cliff waited at one exit for an hour, Harry at the other. Neither knew there were two exits. Eventually Cliff gave up and drove to Suffolk. The team held its breath. What would it be like to play without Harry? One or two of the old lags, who had known nothing else all their adult lives, began to get a little light-headed. Old knee injuries miraculously healed. Ageing fielders bounded across the outfield like twenty-year-olds. Then, at about 3.15, Harry turned up in a cab. His journey had cost him over £70.

Illness and injury are nothing to Harry. In the early days, plots were frequently hatched to stop him turning up. None of them ever worked. We even toyed with kidnapping at one point. The only serious threat to his 100 per cent record came after he and I had left university and granted temporary control of the team to Brian Warr, an immensely bright and eccentric theoretical physicist. As befits a man of vast intelligence, Brian was almost

irresponsibly mischievous. To him, Harry's record represented an irresistible challenge. He therefore arranged
a number of midweek fixtures during the Oxford term,
knowing that Harry had a nine-to-five job in London
and could not easily take days off. Indeed, there was
only one game he could make. That spring, however,
the weather was dreadful. The high moisture content
that habitually bedevils Oxford precipitated an almost
permanent downfall. The one game Harry could make
went ahead. All the others were rained off.

Nowadays everyone accepts Harry's obsession – sometimes, I think, a little too easily. He is a man with
frightening reserves of energy and clear ideas of what
he wants to do with it. Perhaps unusually for a cricket
obsessive, he is crazy about the team rather than the game.
When he and I talk cricket, which we do constantly, we talk
Scott. In 1994, at the age of thirty-four, he played his 365th
game, and so completed a full calender year for Scott. He
is as aware as anyone how sad this is, but he wouldn't have
it any other way. Every successful club needs a Harry. It is
just our luck that we have one of the Harriest.

Next to such awesome statistics, the rest of us look like
dilettantes. Of those 393 games since 1979, Terence has
played 282, and on 252 I am a distant third. Richard had
two years off for good behaviour, but has still notched up
214. In all twelve players have reached a hundred games,
and there are two in the nineties. All bar one are between
thirty-two and thirty-six years old. These people have known
each other an awfully long time.

*   *   *

The journey to the pub is uneventful, interrupted only by a contraflow on the M40 and some whingeing from Terence because I have put him at number 11 again. Rattling through the countryside in Terence's company car, we lapse into silence as I look forward to the first drink of the day and Terence looks forward to not paying for it. This is an old, personal battle, fought over many years in many hundreds of pubs, but I am tempted to use the word 'microcosm' here, for, sadly, round-avoidance is endemic to social cricket. Team members divide neatly and predictably into those who offer to buy everyone a drink and those who resent buying anyone a packet of crisps. Perhaps this sounds trivial. It is trivial, but that doesn't mean it doesn't matter. To ignore round-avoidance would be to play into the hands of these snivelling, grasping cheese-parers. Like businessmen who pick their noses in heavy traffic, round-avoiders always think they can get away with it. They fail to realise that their stratagems are so transparent, and their wallets so patently full of crispy ten-pound notes, that we identify them instantly for what they are. Such minor considerations can drive giant wedges into the social fabric of a cricket team and generate all sorts of disastrous run-outs and lbw decisions later on.

Like any sport, it's all a matter of technique. Skin-flint A walks into the pub, fails to notice that anyone else has arrived, because he's a little short-sighted, and heads straight for the bar. Only when he's bought his Coke does his eyesight miraculously improve. You would think he might see all those people glaring furiously at him as he nibbles his dry-roasted peanuts, but he doesn't.

Skinflint B enters the pub thirty seconds after someone who is noted for his generosity. Diligent observation over many years has failed to determine precisely how he manages to do this. One theory, as yet untested, is that he waits in his car until a suitably philanthropic team-mate arrives. Skinflint B then offers to buy everyone a drink in the knowledge that everyone will say no thanks, Bob's getting me one. With a bit of luck, Bob will get him one too.

Skinflint C waits until everyone has bought a round except for him and Skinflint D. When D finally gives in and asks if anyone would like a drink (when three players are in the loo), C sidles up to him and suggests they split the round. Neither of them buy drinks for himself. The real old hand at the round-avoidance game, however, is Skinflint T, or 'Terence', as he is known. Skinflint T walks into the pub and instantly makes a great show of ordering food, making it clear that the purchase of drinks is a peripheral matter, of no interest to him at this important moment. Strange, though, that this never quite stops him buying one for himself.

Speaking of food, we now remember that it is lunchtime. The rumble of empty stomachs reverberates through the stonework of the pub like a minor earth tremor. The generous forms of our more prosperous players, used to daily business lunches to keep them from flagging, begin to emit strange moans of hunger which, to the untutored ear, sound not unlike whale song. Menus are hurriedly sought. All athletes at the peak of their physical prowess know the importance of regular troughing, and we are no exception. Breakfast was three hours ago. Tea is three hours hence. Without input, there can be no output. Our bodies are well-oiled machines, in need of constant refuelling. The average pub lunch therefore consists of three pints of Löwenbräu, a large microwaved lasagne with chips and a side salad, two packets of barbecue-flavoured crisps, someone else's slightly hotter chips when nobody's looking, and a bar of Cadbury's Dairy Milk for later. If someone is watching his weight, he'll leave out the salad.

So cheerful is the general mood, especially after Skinflint T has been bullied into buying an enormous round, that it almost seems a shame to spoil it by playing cricket. Steve Mills, who is Australian, is keen to get going, but everyone else has that look of post-trough euphoria that would be best dispelled by a nice long nap. Still, the match is due to begin at 2.30, so as captain I lead a small advance party, which arrives at the ground at 2.29. At least three team members have just bought drinks when it is time to go, and Neal's lunch hasn't arrived. Another two players have yet to be seen at all. Howard, our dashing number 3 batsman, never turns up before 2.50, having overslept, underestimated the journey time and taken the wrong exit off the motorway. Charlie 'Dinner Party' Williams has been at a lunch party in Hampshire. He will later leave at 6.30 to go to a dinner party.

I survey Chuffington Magna's scenic home ground. Set against the rolling hills of the Cotswolds, its surrounding foliage is lush and luxuriant. Amiable cows moo in the distance. The calming aroma of excrement wafts rurally across from square leg. Attractive low-flying military aircraft strafe the outfield. A rusting caravan squats elegantly in a nearby ditch.

I change into my whites and don the fearsome Captain Scott cap. This magnificent artefact, with its viciously bright yellow and navy blue stripes, terrifies dogs and is best avoided by anyone with a history of epilepsy in the family. In fact we bought them as a joke, but even jokes can gain a momentum of their own. The standard model features the team motto above a motif of someone being bowled middle stump, all against a yellow background. Being shamelessly elitist, we have recently introduced a second cap for life members – those twelve of us who have played a hundred games or more. This has the same motif and stripes, but features a different motto (*Semper Tristes*' – 'always sad') on a blue background. When we're all wearing them, the effect is very nearly impressive.

Whoever invented the cricket cap did a wonderful thing. A cap says more about you than a sun hat ever can. Let us not forget that the whole Bodyline crisis of 1932–3 might never have erupted had the Australian public not taken such a strong dislike to Douglas Jardine's Harlequins' cap four years earlier. They could not believe that someone would choose to wear a club cap while playing for his country, especially one as outrageously snobby as the Harlequins' multi-coloured number. Thus was born Australia's hatred of Jardine, which begat Jardine's hatred of Australia, which begat Bodyline, which begat, to date, sixty years of non-stop whingeing from the Australians.

Even today, wearing an unfamiliar cap is a marvellous way of putting the wind up the opposition. It identifies you as a complete pseud, true, but people still assume you are a better player for it. Scotties moonlighting for other teams often find that they bat much higher up the order if they don their retina-searing Modo Egrediors. Somehow the mere possession of such an item automatically confers great talent upon its wearer. And the stupider the cap, the more talented everyone thinks you are. As fair-minded people, we should probably correct such inaccurate impressions. We should be willing to play within our own limitations as cricketers, rather than relying on the curious mystique of our lurid headwear. But sod that. To be treated with the respect you aren't due is the dream of every talentless sportsman. The raw power of a multi-coloured cricket cap cannot be overestimated.

Now to identify the opposition captain and introduce myself. Unless we have met many times before, we shall both instantly forget each other's names and have to address each other as 'Skip' for the rest of the afternoon. By a quarter to three most of our team have arrived, except for Howard, of course, and Harry is looking for someone to help him carry the kit into the dressing room. Everyone vanishes. Harry says he is sick of this and is going to leave the kit in the boot. Players re-emerge from hiding. I myself am too busy psyching myself up for the toss to offer much assistance. Harry has a quick look at the wicket and says we should bowl. The other side are strong, he says, and we should already be thinking about the draw. There might be a little early life in the wicket which we should take advantage of. Everybody else in the team, however, wants to bat, because it's a nice day and they fancy a lie-down. Upon such vital considerations are tactical decisions frequently based.

I walk out to the wicket with the opposing captain, apologising in advance that we are a bit weaker than usual. If we genuinely are a bit weaker than usual, this is a plea from the heart. Be gentle with us. Please don't crush us into the dirt. Otherwise it is just an underhand attempt to lull him into a false sense of security. It is crucial to define the terms of the game before you get going: not just whether you will play limited overs or declaration, but which one of you wants to win more than the other and how unscrupulous he intends to be to achieve that victory. Unless the needle in the fixture has reached unmanageable proportions, I would always prefer a good close game to a rampant fuck-you victory. Most opposing captains, fortunately, are on a similar wavelength. Only a few are more singleminded. If Skip has a strange glint in his eye when he assures me that they too are a little under strength today, I know immediately that we are going to be murdered. Captains need to be competitive: the will to win is an entirely natural one. But some men accept the captaincy of their team as a consolation for their inability to achieve other more personally fulfilling career ambitions, such as invading Poland. This is the sort of captain who uses his two best bowlers for 16 overs each, by which time we're 53 for 7 and want to go home.

So we stand at the crease, grinning at each other,

certain that we have correctly assessed each other's levels of moral probity and competence, while Skip tosses his double-headed coin. 'Tails,' I call, having called heads incorrectly every Sunday since 1988. 'Hmm,' he says, studying the unseasonably blue sky and the surprisingly flat wicket. 'I think we'll bat.' I return to tell everyone the bad news.

Captaincy is a subtle art, requiring tactical insight, man-management skills, a firm chin, endless patience and a powerful set of lungs. Many hundreds of books have been written on the subject. Sometimes I feel as though I have read them all. Perhaps the best and certainly the most authoritative is Mike Brearley's *The Art of Captaincy*, mainly because when Brearley wrote it, he had skilfully fostered a reputation for having the largest brain in the world. It may be cleverer to be thought clever than to be clever, and to be thought to be as clever as Brearley is very clever indeed. But as his book shows, Brearley only knew the half of it. He was a superb Test captain, undoubtedly, with a deep understanding of the way people tick, and an instinctive knowledge of how to get the best out of unlikely raw material. But when did he ever have to collect tea money? When did he ever have to go to the opposition's skipper and say, 'Er, look, I'm terribly sorry, but we seem to have an extra man by mistake. Would it be all right if we played twelve-a-side?'

For it is out here, in the uncompromising world of 'friendly' cricket, that a captain really earns his spurs. Anyone can marshal the world's best cricketers into a

series-winning fighting force. But I can't imagine that
Michael Atherton has ever had to ring around all his
friends on the first morning of a Test match because
Graeme Hick has been told by his wife that he has to
put up some shelves.

The perfect illustration of this disparity is the phenom-
enon of 'stonedrift'. It has different names in different
teams, but whatever it is called, stonedrift makes the life
of every captain at village level a waking hell. In our team
it was named after Paul Stone, an early stalwart and a
master of the practice. You would ask him to field at
cover point. Off he would trot, smiling and eager to
please (thoroughly nice fellow, Paul, always smiling and
eager to please). Ten minutes later you would glance over
to cover point, expecting to see Paul Stone, hoping to see
Paul Stone, sometimes praying to see Paul Stone. But at
cover point there was an uncanny absence of Paul Stones.
Not one Paul Stone was there to be seen. Sometimes he had
drifted off to the third-man boundary, sometimes to short
mid-off. Invariably he had completely forgotten where he
was supposed to be. Once he made it as far as square leg.
But he would still be smiling – and so were the batsmen,
as they clumped every ball through the convenient hole
in the field. Paul Stone drifted off completely a few years
ago, but his legacy remains. Some fielders stonedrift with
astounding skill and timing, often disappearing from their
allotted position only seconds before the batsman offers
them an easy catch there. Sometimes they move closer
to someone else to have a chat. Or perhaps there is a
left-hander in and they can't remember where they have

to go. Some fielders can only remember two positions, one for each end, and when you want them to be in different places for each batsman, a form of intellectual short-circuit takes place and they wander around like long-stay mental hospital patients recently released into the community. And yet in our team many stonedrifters have been playing cricket regularly for fifteen years. When you try to move them back to the position you first put them in, they look utterly dumbfounded, and sometimes throw up their arms in despair, as if to say that you really should make up your mind. In fact, you already have made up your mind – to absentmindedly stab them with your fork during the tea interval.

These are the real issues of captaincy. It is unlikely that, during his long career, Allan Border ever turned up at a Test match ground with only ten men and had to borrow someone's small son who couldn't catch, throw, bat or bowl in order to make up the numbers. When first-class captains try to hide someone in the field, it's probably only because he can't throw a ball 60 yards flat to the wicketkeeper while still lying on the ground having dived 15 yards to stop a certain 4 just inside the rope. In Captain Scott I am trying to hide fielders who will duck if the ball comes anywhere near them. We put people in the slips not because they might take a slip catch – please, be sensible – but because there they are out of harm's way.

Of course, professional captains don't have it totally easy. They have to keep their players motivated and performing to their full potential. They have to be inventive and courageous in the field. If they lose, it's their fault, and if they carry on losing, they get fired. No one can fire me or Harry: I'm the signatory to the team's bank account, and he has all the kit.

And at least we never have to justify any of our actions to the press. 'So can you tell me why you continued to bowl Martin Dyckhoff after he conceded 35 from his first 3 overs?'

'Well, he didn't bowl much last week, and I'm planning to put him in at number 10.'

'And what about your own three dropped catches and two-ball 0? Do you feel your own place may be in doubt?'

No, I think the glare of publicity is probably something we can do without.

And so, after all the preparation, the toss, the usual arguments in the dressing room and the triumphant arrival of Howard, who had taken the right exit but the wrong motorway, we wander out on to the field, a mere twenty-three minutes after the scheduled start of the game. I am opening the bowling with our steadiest bowler and our most fragile bowler: the latter because when he starts getting hit around, his head drops and you may as well take him off, and because opening batsmen are less likely to hit him around; and the former because of the latter. Neither is actually the fastest we have: that honour belongs to Tim the perennially angry fast bowler, who will be rendered even angrier by being relegated to first change. Very nearly as furious will be Martin, our ex-fast bowler, who used to open the bowling but whose shock value – the bowler who once bowled fast, and looks as though he bowls fast, but doesn't bowl fast at all – is now best utilised against the tail. Arvind the lubricious solicitor prefers first change anyway. Bowler number 6 will be one of several humorous spinners whose spell will drastically increase the opposition's scoring rate.

By mid-afternoon those steak and kidney pies have taken their toll. Fielders who in ideal conditions would sprint around the boundary like gazelles are now bouncing around like unruly spacehoppers. The runs flow off the bat. When, by some terrible misjudgement, someone occasionally gets out, the new batsman virtually sprints to the crease, so keen is he to help himself. Perhaps it's that dangerous combination of slowish medium-pace bowling on a flat wicket with an old ball (we have run out of new balls, so the village has palmed us off with something that looks like an old slipper) to geriatric fielders that has so galvanised the opposition today. By tea Chuffington Magna have scored 212 for 5. A sneering young Jason with too much hair gel has scored 86 not out, hitting everything to the leg side. Our bowlers bowl everything on the leg side anyway, so that's all right. We pray that they won't bat on after tea. It will be hard enough to get 213 anyway. For the tea is massive, and the players are looking peckish again.

It doesn't matter how much you had for lunch. A doughnut is a doughnut. Similarly, cheese and pickle sandwiches are cheese and pickle sandwiches. Some cricketers live for tea, and many judge a fixture entirely by the quality of the tea that accompanies it. Generally, home-made chocolate cakes are considered acceptable, as are eggy sandwiches, lots of pickle in the cheese and pickle sandwiches, those chocolate cornflake or rice krispie things (fondly remembered from the 1970s), home-made jam tarts, banana sandwiches, scones and jam, Mr Kipling's rich chocolate slices and anything with cream on. Beetroot and salad, popular in odd corners of Hampshire, are less well received. Cricket teas are the great reversion to childhood. If there were jelly on the table, you can be sure it would be consumed with alacrity. Spiritual balloons hang from the wall, and sometimes you have to fight the overwhelming instinct to set up a game of Pin the Tail on the Donkey. This is why most teams will do virtually anything to stop their womenfolk joining them for tea. Consider these points.

1: The first person to the table sits directly in front of the largest plate of cakes.

2: Everyone takes a handful of sandwiches as well as a cake, having been well brought up.

3: Everyone eats the sandwiches before the cakes.

4: All the doughnuts have disappeared before the last player has come in off the field.

5: People don't say, 'Does anyone want this last banana sandwich?' as they would normally do in adult company. They just take it.

6: If there are any Club biscuits, at least one person will sing, 'If you like a lot of chocolate on your biscuit join our club.'

Cricketers don't want to be seen like this. They know that one cricket tea would confirm every prejudice women have ever held about male behaviour patterns. Hard-won respect would be destroyed in a moment. Who can blame men from trying to exclude their wives and girlfriends from such dangerous knowledge? Besides, they would probably eat all the best cakes.

What this all means in the short term is that, after tea, no one can walk again. Chuffington's bright-eyed young warriors have eschewed the rock cakes and nibbled daintily at the doughnuts. At our end of the table scarcely a molecule of food has survived. As I write down the batting order, and then rush out to umpire before everyone starts complaining, I know that this is going to be one of those innings. No singles, because there is no guarantee that the opening batsmen will make it to the other end alive. No 4s, because they aren't up to it. No runs at all, in fact, which will wake up the rest of the team, for nothing excites their ire more than opening batsmen playing slowly. Soon some suitably fearless umpire will be sent out to wag the finger and dispose of the offending blockers. Then everyone else will pour in, try to play shots too early, get out and leave us 68 for 6 at 6.30, when the 20 overs start. We shall play for the draw, and if Terence and Martin and I can stay in for a while, we shall probably get it. Then we will all go to the pub where the recriminations will start.

And so it goes. My thirty-five minute 0 not out is the talk of the county, while Terence's fearless four-ball 11 not out has given at least half the team heart seizures and the other half, who did not bet on how many balls he would survive, a huge laugh. We troop off, and I shake hands with Skip, thanking him for a splendid game and asking him how much the tea money is. Harry is filling in all the gaps in the scorebook, while other players lean over him and point out that those two leg byes should have been down as two runs, the umpire agreed he had made a mistake, look do you want to ask him? In the dressing room there is silence: everyone is too tired to talk. The shower-takers have stripped off and are waving their equipment around with the lack of inhibition that so often characterises the physically repulsive. The shower-avoiders are trying not to look too smelly. Some players are changing as quickly as possible in order to charge off to the pub and so avoid repacking the kit. Charlie 'Dinner Party' Williams has left for his dinner party. One or two want to be back in London before the traffic gets heavy (got an early meeting tomorrow). One erroneously told his wife he would be back by seven o'clock. Harry is still completing the match statistics, and shouts, 'Can someone pack up the kit, please?' Most people affect not to hear. I am still scrounging around for tea money. One player says he has his money in the car, but when he finally gets to the car, forgets about the tea money and drives off.

And so to the pub, without about a third of the kit we started out with. Another magnificent day's cricket has come to an end. We sit and exchange gossip, idly wondering who among the team has the ugliest children. Someone suggests that we all go for a curry, just as we always used to. No one responds. We are all exhausted, and those doughnuts will trouble our digestive systems for some hours to come. Tomorrow, headaches, indigestion, ennui, muscular spasms. Next weekend, the same thing all over again.

CHAPTER EIGHT

The Complete A to Z of Captain Scott Batsmanship

Our failure in the Chuffington Magna game will probably have seemed unforgivably supine and spineless to the inexperienced reader, but more weathered competitors will understand the appalling pressures a side like ours can face. Like a lot of teams, we are never more likely to fail than when we think we might do well. We are also never more likely to fail than when we know we are going to do badly. Put bluntly, we are never more likely to fail than when we take part at all. Only by complete non-participation do we have any chance of retaining our self-respect. For the discipline of batting can make demands on us that even our close relatives would regard as excessive. Questions of style and content compete with questions of physical bravery, intellectual acuity and spiritual strength, while a strong pair of pads also helps. It's all a matter of confidence, and more precisely, of not looking a complete idiot. What you don't want is people to say 'Well batted' when all you did was stick around for half a dozen overs while someone else had all the fun. You want respect, not pity. Sadly, after sixteen years of trying, I have graduated only as far as sympathy, although I can think of at least one person on the team who doesn't even get that. What I have learned is that there is more to batting than mere batting. There are countless other factors to be taken into consideration, none of which you will find in a training manual. What is needed is a guide to all these extraneous factors, a guide which is easy to assimilate and which can be quickly referred to before that all-important match-losing innings. What is needed, in other words, is the Complete A to Z of Captain Scott Batsmanship.

A – Attire

Vitally important when it comes to creating the right impression with the opposition. As well as your humor-ously multi-coloured cap, be sure to wear old-fashioned cream-coloured trousers for that toured-Australia-in-the-1950s look. Manmade materials are for people who play in leagues or sell insurance over the telephone. Shirtsleeves must also be judged to perfection. If you have big, tanned arms and wish to give the impression of great physical strength, go for a short-sleeved shirt, and flex your biceps between balls. Weeds have fewer options, but can at least try to look dashing and elegant by wearing a long-sleeved shirt with the sleeves rolled up to just below the elbow. This conceals those non-existent biceps while giving you an air of E.R. Dexter-style devil-may-care amateurism, as opposed to mere amateurism. Cravats show a certain wit, but against a fast bowler with a chip on his shoulder, they might precipitate a lengthy spell in hospital.

B – Backing Up

There are two schools of thought here, as represented for the purposes of this discussion by the crazed Cliff and Arvind, our solicitor from Delhi. As the bowler comes into bowl, Cliff jumps around in the crease as though someone has recently introduced a swarm of bees to his trousers. The ball proceeds from the bowler's hand in the normal way, but as it moves in the direction of the batsman, the chances are that Cliff will overtake it as he seeks to gain an advantage on the first run. Often this urge to take a quick single fails to take into account the relative speed of the other batsman, which means that Cliff may be completing a second run before his more sedate partner has managed his first. Fortunately, Cliff will usually sneak in a third before anyone has noticed.

Arvind has a more puritanical approach. When he is facing, quick singles are mandatory, even if he doesn't quite get round to calling before sprinting up the pitch in your direction. But when backing up, Arvind becomes strangely immobile, achieving a state of such inner calm that even in an emergency he remains entirely unaware of all your shouts of 'Yes!', 'Quick one, Arvind!' and 'Get a move on, you fat cunt!' It's as though he has spent many years reflecting on the relative significance of different people's runs, and has concluded, after due consideration, that his must take priority. To bat next to Arvind in the order is to be run out for 0 without facing a ball. Rumours that certain players in the team are attempting to have his visa rescinded have yet to be confirmed.

C – Chinese Cut

To some, a surefire sign that the batsman hasn't a clue what he's doing. To others (i.e., the batsman), an ingenious example of last-minute improvisation that surprises everyone except, of course, the batsman himself. Quadruple these reactions if the ball contrives to cross the boundary.

Even non-cricketers, though, have heard of the Chinese cut, and everyone knows all the silly names for the shot (Harrow drive, etc.). This tends to deflect attention from any number of other run-acquiring false shots which lack silly names but are just as rib-tickling. The failed on-drive, for instance, that fizzes helplessly through the air down to third man. Few captains set a field for this shot, having either put third man deep to hide a bad fielder or not bothered with one at all because that's what Mike Atherton does. My own favourite false shot is the edged outswinger ingeniously placed between first slip and wicketkeeper, so that both of them glare at each other for missing such an easy chance. Another goody is the failed Robin Smith slam-dunk crashing square drive that flies over the wicketkeeper's head for 4. 'It's all runs in the book,' says Geoffrey Boycott. 'It doesn't matter how you get them.' And what a popular man he is.

D – Dry, Hanging the Bat Out to

A triumph of instinct over common sense, and the bane of every batsman's life. The ball is perhaps a little short of a length, fast and safely wide. So what do you do? You could always leave it, ideally with the great Brearley flourish that has now, for some reason, fallen out of favour. Alternatively, you could get in line and play a wristy back-foot slash just to let the bowler know who's in charge. But instead you just feebly prod your bat at the ball, protecting neither body nor stumps but just nibbling it straight to the wicketkeeper. It's such an undignified shot, and in a Test match it would mean instant dismissal. In village cricket, fortunately, there is an estimated 32 per cent probability that the wicketkeeper enjoyed too large a lunch to catch it cleanly, and a 26 per cent chance that the regular 'keeper couldn't make it and someone else is standing in. But beware, for if you're out, there is a 38 per cent probability that you will tell your team-mates you had to be playing well just to get a touch, and a 97 per cent

chance that someone will then punch you in the mouth.
Who said cricket statistics were boring?

E – Entrance, Making an

Out you stride, centre-stage, the next man in, checking you
haven't forgotten anything important, like your bat, and
noticing just in time that your flies are undone. Taking
guard is another opportunity to show the opposition who's
boss. Harry, our opening batsman and blockmeister, takes
guard 2½ feet outside the crease, which, when the bowler
is walking 30 yards back to his mark, appears to be an act
of some bravery. The real reason is that Harry has become
paranoid about being given out lbw on the front foot by
incompetent umpires, but the bowler doesn't know that.
(As it is, most incompetent umpires are far too dozy to
notice that Harry has taken his guard so far up the wicket,
and give him out lbw anyway.) Ian Wall, the most violent
hitter we have, has the enormous advantage of being taller
and broader than most opposition teams put together, so
when he takes his guard he does so by making the tiniest
of indentations in the crease, and immediately turning
to the bowler. This means that within 0.8 seconds he is
ready to face his first ball, making it clear that he doesn't
care where the field has been placed or what the bowler
is going to bowl. Even if teams do not quail before his
mighty bulk, they're usually impressed by this display of
casual arrogance.

Rather less intimidating is the batsman for whom taking

guard is a ritual of almost archaeological significance. For such a batsman the bat is not something to hit the ball with, it's an ersatz shovel. Down and down he digs, carefully forming that strange W shape that he once read about in a training manual. After about twenty minutes he's finally ready – except that now play has to be suspended because a giant duststorm is blowing through square leg. He stands up and, with great deliberation, surveys the field. He looks cover point straight in the eye. He has been on a management course where he was told to do that. He settles down, moves his feet into position, pats his bat on the ground. Then, as the bowler sprints in, he stands up again and holds up his hand, dramatically stopping the bowler in his tracks. Perhaps he has a speck of grit in his eye. Or perhaps second slip coughed, disturbing his concentration. It is all quite pointless, for as everyone around the ground knows, this batsman will be out within three balls. So many years has he spent practising taking guard that he has forgotten how to bat. If by luck he does survive, he will make you pay for it, for every ten minutes he will lose his mark and go through the rigmarole all over again.

F – Forward Defensive

The first stroke a batsman is taught, and the first stroke he forgets. 'There was nothing I could do about it,' bewailed one of our demon fast bowlers the other day, having been bowled first ball by a perfectly pitched-up straight one. 'You could try a forward defensive,' I suggested, at which he stared at me blankly. Why play a defensive shot when you could try to propel the offending ball out of the ground with the force of a small nuclear device? For such a batsman a defensive shot is an admission of defeat. He forgets that Viv Richards invariably played a defensive shot after hitting a 6, knowing that it doesn't pay to tempt fate too often. But what was good enough for the greatest stroke-player of the age is not good enough for Captain Scott's number 10 long-eared bunny rabbit. The match situation is tense. There are 12 overs left. We are hanging on, as usual, for a stubborn, nasty little draw. The pitch is playing well; the batsmen, sadly, are not. All our hero needs to do is settle down, play himself in, try to keep the bowlers out, try to stop them doing to him what in other circumstances he would be trying to do to them. So what happens? He takes a huge agricultural mow at his first ball and is bowled middle stump.

Of course, you can go too far the other way, as Harry proves in virtually every match. Never is a long hop ever quite long enough, nor a half-volley as half as it could be. True, he has the backward defensive stroke as a variation, but you know his heart isn't in it. The forward defensive is his masterpiece. He is the Leonardo of the soft-handed prod, and his Mona Lisa smile as another loose ball is nullified shows the satisfaction to be gained from a job well done. It's much as the rest of us feel, in fact, after we have let down his tyres.

G – Gardening

Too little too late in most cases. If you're playing on a dodgy village pitch and a ball flies up at you, is there any point prodding the field where it landed? Is it not a clear sign to the opposition that you're a bit of a git? Usually the only thing that will improve such pitches is concentrated mortar fire. Stay in the crease and concentrate on keeping out the grubber to come.

H – Helmet

Another serious mistake. In 1994 one of our opponents came out to bat in a helmet, with the tortured air of a man who has recently been caught molesting farm animals. Disturbed by our snorts of derision, he explained that the previous week he had fractured his cheekbone. 'You're a brave man to play again so soon,' sympathised our fastest bowler, before bowling six bouncers at him in a row.

I – Injuries

As ever, there are good injuries and bad injuries to have, depending mainly on one's perceived dignity level (PDL) after the event. Tearing or wrenching or pulling or aggravating or straining something important has a very high PDL, ranging up to the maximum for the 'old cartilage injury' that speaks of a solidly athletic past. On the face of it the exalted status of the old cartilage injury is absurd, as the implication is that without surgery you may never walk again. But this doesn't stop one able if ageing Scott batsman from invoking it constantly. Fifty or 60 not out, and the twinge arrives just as he's beginning to baulk at the quick singles. A runner goes out, and Jonathan happily carries on smashing bowlers around while the poor runner does all the legwork. Fortunately, the old cartilage injury usually clears up in time for him to bowl 5 overs later on.

Other injuries carry less kudos. Being hit on the head by a fast bowler and waking up in intensive care scores only a low PDL, especially if you fell unconscious outside the crease and the bastards ran you out. And being hit in the testicles because you forgot to wear a box is just pathetic. You are writhing in agony, and everyone else is in hysterics. Should you leave the field, on the otherwise reasonable grounds that you need emergency surgery, you'll be laughed at for the rest of your life, although not by your children, because you will never be able to have any. It is a rare batsman who forgets his box more than once.

J – Jaunty Air

A great way to annoy the opposition, this, especially if they're those taciturn types who believe that even a 35-over Sunday afternoon knockabout should be played deadly seriously. Chatting to miserable wicketkeepers, and keeping up a constant commentary on everything that takes place, can often lead to such concerted attempts to get you out that the bowling falls to pieces and you can score tons of runs. Look at Derek Randall's effect on the Australians in the Centenary Test of 1976–7. As he amassed his epic (and nearly match-winning) 174, no one suffered more than the Australian wicketkeeper, Rodney Marsh. Hour after hour of jaunty comments and fidgeting and 'Come on, Rags' every twenty seconds drove him to the very precipice of sanity. Here was a man who, in the right circumstances, could have performed terrible deeds upon Randall's person. Only self-control of Olympian standards, as well as the knowledge that it was on live television and his defence lawyer wouldn't have a leg to stand on, prevented him. Randall's achievement should be a lesson to us all.

K – Kit

Even at the humblest, most incompetent level, batting is all in the mind, and the availability or otherwise of acceptable kit can cruelly sabotage the batsman's elusive mental balance. For years we have lugged around two gigantic bags full of rotting, malodorous pads, bats and left-handed gloves, and most people dip into it regularly. Why all the gloves are left-handed, no one knows. We begin the season with several pairs of bright shiny new right-handed gloves, but as the summer progresses these all disappear, and we gain about half a dozen pairs of left-handed gloves from other teams. The cries of torment as the next batsman in searches desperately for the last matching right-handed pair are a regular feature of our late-summer games.

Some players buy their own kit, but therein lie further pitfalls. If someone has a good season, your heart sinks when he turns up the following April with his own brand-new bat, bought at frightening expense from Lillywhites and decorated with some magnificent number like '405', '333' or, most recently, '501'. Never trust a bat with a large number on it, because you will never score as many runs with it in your whole life. If Gray–Nicolls or Gunn & Moore created a bat called '3 not out', I might buy it. Otherwise, forget it. For after the hopeful purchase, the owner of this magnificent new blade loses form so absolutely that by mid-June he has usually taken up golf. The new bat simply hates being used for more than three or four balls at a time 'I'm playing it in,' the batsman explains after another 0. He perseveres. He has spent £100 on this bat, and he is going to get his money's worth. Then one day someone else picks it up by mistake and scores a lightning 50. 'Brilliant bat you've got here,' he beams. The owner sobs into his tea, goes back to the bat he used last season and the runs begin to flow once more.

The one item of personal kit that I wouldn't be without, though, is my own box. We have already discussed the parlous consequences of batting without one of these essential items. But the only alternative, if you don't have one of your own, is a communal box. Many of my team-mates I have known for a decade or more; some of them I feel I know quite well. But can anyone truly claim to know anyone who willingly uses a communal box? In the kitbags fester around eight of these ancient artefacts, all slightly greasy to the touch and, in every weather, suspiciously warm. Nothing can destroy my enjoyment of a game more effectively than the discovery that I have forgotten or lost my box. With trepidation I approach the box bag and try to select the one least likely to have seen intimate service in the preceding couple of hours. Every ball I face (and they tend to be few in number) I cannot overcome the knowledge that this foreign body lurks within my trousers. And yet some players blithely undergo this nightmare week after week. Do their wives know?

L – Leg Byes

The batsman's most hated extra, as he is inevitably convinced he hit it. Watch for the signals to the scorer as he reaches the other end: the index finger pointing at the bat, the index finger pointing at the umpire, the index finger and thumb joined at the ends to indicate that the umpire is a wanker. Then watch for the umpire raising his own index finger at the very next opportunity.

M – Maiden

There are two views of this: the batsman is proud that he has just survived an over of vicious, unplayable deliveries, while his team-mates regard him as feeble, pusillanimous and selfish for overlooking six such succulent scoring opportunities. There is no known way of reconciling the two.

N – No-Ball

A lovely idea: the bowler oversteps, the umpire shouts 'No-ball!' and the batsman rivets the ball for 6. In practice the umpire probably won't notice that it's a no-ball, and the batsman will be bowled. Or he will call it, but so late that the batsman can't adjust his shot, and he will look stupid. Or the batsman will adjust his shot, cream it through the covers and be so excited by the whole process that he'll run himself out coming back for a third. Not really worth the effort.

O – Off Stump, Fishing Outside the

See D for Dry, Hanging the Bat Out to.

P – Playing Yourself In

A delightful practice, reserved only for top-order batsmen at the beginning of the innings. Middle-order batsmen are all supposed to be wildly attacking anyway, while lower-order batsmen are cannon fodder whose role is to make up for the mistakes the top-order batsmen made while playing themselves in for twenty-five overs. The only feasible solution is carefully staged car accidents.

Q – Quick Exit

Style is everything when you're out. Some of the angrier players glare at the umpire or the bat or the stumps but never, for some reason, into the mirror, where the true cause of their downfall lies. Well supplied as we are with players who know their own minds, vicious arguments have often been known to ensue, which usually means the end of another attractive fixture. How much more sensible to follow the example of my friend Richard, who regards a quick exit as the most dignified gesture a batsman can make. Pausing a split-second for a pang of self-disgust, he whips the bat under his arm and turns for the pavilion in one seamless movement. In the past couple of years Richard's batting has suffered something of a decline, but his exits are more polished than ever, and sometimes he's off before the opposition can even shout 'Howzat?' The Australians in the team consider him a basket case. Richard also has strong opinions about walking, having once, on a notorious occasion, walked on an lbw. When umpiring he operates on the assumption that a gentleman will always walk, a sad delusion which gives rise to some strong exchanges of opinion in the pub later. Tim wouldn't walk if he were bowled. Harry is so obsessed with the low standards of umpiring – particularly in the matter of front-foot lbws – that he assumes all umpires are wrong as a matter of course, except when he's umpiring and never gives out any batsmen in any circumstances.

R – *Retired Hurt*

When does retired hurt mean retired hurt? Whenever it doesn't mean retired knackered, retired bored or retired keen-to-protect-the-average-against-all-comers. As a means of annoying everyone on the field, it's fireproof. One deeply pedestrian batsman, whose skills do not extend to willingly giving up his wicket, occasionally retires on 50 and insists on counting this as not out, despite much complaint from everyone else and at least one petition to Lord's. Another more skilled batsman, for whom centuries represent a normal day at the office, usually trots off as soon as he has reached three figures. 'Thought I'd give someone else a go,' he lies on his return. Opposition bowlers are annoyed because they suspect that the gesture shows a certain level of contempt for their efforts. Team-mates are annoyed because the retirer has chosen to withdraw his labour just as the opening bowlers are coming back for a final blast fifteen minutes before tea. This doesn't give anyone else a go, it gives them an opportunity to get out for 0. Many Scott batsmen grasp this opportunity with both hands.

S – Strike, Farming the

Always done with the best of intentions, e.g., to protect the incoming batsman from the most dangerous bowler. What actually happens is that the well-set batsman keeps all the easy strike for himself and ensures that the other batsman faces the demon at the other end, turning down all calls for a single should this cosy status quo be threatened. If both bowlers are rubbish, singles miraculously become available on the sixth ball of every over. When challenged later, strike-farmers usually claim that it was for the good of the team. Run out the bastard the first chance you get.

T – Throwing the Bat

1: As in selflessly launching your trusty blade at any ball in order to gain quick runs after your stodgy opening batsman has spent 35 overs scoring 28. It's even worse when the stodgy opening batsman is also the captain, as frequently happens with us. To be told to sacrifice oneself needlessly after two hours of strokeless purgatory can provoke the most mild-mannered of middle-order batsmen, which may have something to do with those dodgy front-foot lbw decisions I mentioned earlier.

2: As in projecting the offending implement across the crowded dressing room after being out for 0 for the fifth

match in a row. When Tim is out cheaply, team-mates flee
for the hills.

U – Up Periscope

Standard response when an apparently harmless ball grubs
straight along the ground and hits the middle stump. It is
a matter of record that a batsman who has been out for 0
on Saturday to a ball that lifted viciously off a good length
will be out for 0 on Sunday to an unplayable shooter.
'Why were you playing back?' the team's technique expert
cries, forgetting that yesterday it was only the last-moment
intervention of the corner of your bat that saved you from
troublesome and expensive dental surgery. This time the
ball behaves less like a Rottweiler than a yapping terrier
nipping around your heels, but the result is much the
same. I find that kicking a left-handed glove around the
boundary for half an hour generally resolves all lingering
feelings of frustration.

Council pitches in London are the worst. In most
villages a certain sense of decorum prevents the local
populace from absentmindedly desecrating the cricket
pitch, but in most Greater London boroughs all notions
of public-spiritedness have long since been abandoned.
Rottweilers, yapping terriers and tramps are therefore free
to urinate on a good length, while bowlers' footmarks are
frequently soiled by more substantial obstacles. Perhaps,
given all the other possibilities, getting out for 0 could
well be the easy option.

V – Vengeance

Cricketers never forget. Arvind was recently given out lbw to a ball that would have missed leg stump even if it hadn't pitched outside it and been too high to hit anyway. The umpire was Miserable Bill Matthews, whom Arvind had run out the previous year. Back in the mid-eighties, when our team was rather less proficient than it is now, we were often saved from humiliation by the efforts of a very serious advertising man, who liked to show how serious he was by wearing very silly glasses indeed. One day, though, he gave Neal out in a decision that made even the opposition blench with embarrassment. Fifteen minutes later, the ad man was batting and Neal was umpiring. It was like a gun out of a holster. Wyatt Earp could have been no faster. The ball had scarcely rebounded off the ad-man's pad, four and a half feet down the wicket, before Neal had raised his digit with a grin of triumph you could see from the boundary. The ad-man was incensed. In the changing room he threw an enormous tantrum, donned his amusing glasses and stomped off, vowing never to play for the team again. Strangely enough for an ad-man, he was telling the truth. We have never seen him since.

W – Wide One, Fishing at a

See O for Off Stump, Fishing Outside the.

X – Xcuses

Even if you have no answer to a good ball, you must have an answer to your team-mates.

'It moved a mile.'

'Drifted away and came in off the pitch. You'd have to be Brian Lara to get close to that.'

'I didn't want to say anything, but I think he might be throwing it.'

'Front foot again. Why can't anyone umpire around here?'

'I hit it.'

'I didn't hit it.'

'I called, but he can't have heard me.'

'He was too slow on the first run.'

'He was too fast on the first run.'

'Can't have been out. I was in by miles.'

'Sorry, skipper, I've done my hamstring.'

'Christ, that wicketkeeper's a shit.'

'See the bloke who caught me? Played against Zimbabwe A last week.'

'Bastard bowled right out of the sun.'

Etc. etc. etc.

Y – Yes, No, Yes, No, Yes, Yes, No . . .

Now let's get this straight, shall we? If you wish to run, you shout 'Yes'. If you wish not to run, you shout 'No'. If you're not too sure about it, you shout 'Wait' and pause until your mental processes have caught up with the situation. You do not shout 'Yes, no, yes, no, yes, yes, no' until both batsmen are in the middle of the pitch, or are at the same end. You do not then have a huge row about which one got into the crease first. You do not ask the umpire to intervene, because the umpire does not know the rules, and will give out the one he likes least anyway. You do not call each other rude names, or aim passing sideswipes with your bat. You do not have a blazing argument with each other back in the pavilion. You don't do any of this. You don't? Then come and play for our team. We need you.

Z – Zimmer Frame

It's only a matter of time.

CHAPTER NINE

June

A cold, wet, wintry Thursday in June – and I am safe indoors watching television. Today is the first day of the first Test match, and my entire week has been structured around this moment. It is remarkable, if you really put your mind to it, how much work you can complete before 10.55 am, between 1.00 and 1.40 pm, between 3.40 and 4.00 pm, and after six o'clock, or whenever André Agassi's first-round match starts. During Test matches people all around England are frantically squeezing their lives into these tiny bursts of activity. Indeed, the efficiency and discipline that such a work regime demands can only be to the long-term benefit of British industry as a whole. Alternatively, you can throw a sicky. Migraines, 'flu, gastroenteritis, swine fever, botulism and malaria all strike at fortnightly intervals during the summer, often flooring their victims for anything up to five miserable bedridden days. Six, if there's a rest day.

My own feeling is that supporting the England cricket team is such a stressful activity in itself that fortnightly physical breakdowns are not just possible but inevitable. Several days' rest on the sofa would seem the perfect treatment. In the long term, of course, there is only one practicable solution: chronic idleness. In the early 1980s I endured a long spell of post-graduation unemployment, which did little for my state of mind but enhanced my cricket-viewing opportunities no end. Now, after many years of office-related misery, my life as a faintly underemployed freelance journalist allows me to waste vast swathes of quality time lying in front of the television set screaming abuse at Jack Bannister. You eventually pay the price for such self-indulgence – in bedsores, if nothing else – but for the moment it feels like time well wasted.

So, at 10.50 this fine, thundery morning, as the roofs of cars in the street outside buckle under the force of the rain, I settle into the sofa, relaxed and ready for inaction. *Wisden* is at my side. A huge biscuit barrel nestles within arm's reach. The telephone answering machine is switched on ('Marcus Berkmann is currently on assignment in Angola and cannot be contacted for the foreseeable future'). The fridge is crammed full of snackable comestibles for easy retrieval between overs. At Old Trafford the weather forecast is as gloomy as ever, but at least it looks as though play is going to start on time. The umpires walk sedately out to the middle. The fielders follow thirty seconds later, performing nervous breathing exercises and running up and down on the spot. The batsmen emerge, to expectant applause. And, oh God, first up at the microphone is Jack Bannister.

A long day's television watching can throw up many unconnected thoughts, a substantial proportion of which involve boiling Jack Bannister's lifeless carcass in pure-grade vegetable oil. How one longs for the simple certainties of the Jim Laker era. It was Laker, of course, who introduced to a wider public the phrase 'and he gave that the kitchen sink'. No cricketing expression evokes more precisely the psychopathic bloodlust that overwhelms some batsmen when they spot a slow leg-side long hop fluttering wistfully in their direction. Once or twice a season, the Scotts come up against a batsman who exhibits this very level of violent intent, having recently been released from Broadmoor and now keen to make up for lost time. Flecks of foam spray over the close fielders as he bludgeons the ball to all parts. He doesn't wish to dominate, he wishes to destroy. And at some point during the assault, Harry and I catch each other's eye and mouth the words 'kitchen sink' across the unpopulated outfield. Laker's ghost, commentating from above, would surely approve.

The past ten years have not been kind to the legend of Laker. In death the reputation of many an eminent figure suddenly swells, as all the bores and deadbeats emerge from hiding to praise him with a zeal they would never have dreamed of showing while the poor sod was alive. But Laker has never been 'reassessed', let alone 'rehabilitated'. Decades of thankless commentating appear to have counted for nothing. Laker-related reminiscences now concentrate purely on his 19 wickets in the Old Trafford Test of 1956 – a magnificent achievement, to be sure, but hardly anything to be compared with the coining of the phrase 'and he gave that the kitchen sink'.

Laker's mistake, I suspect, was to stick to TV commentary in an era that has valued more highly the garrulous exhibitionism of *Test Match Special*. It is one of the curiosities of our cricketing culture that the media coverage without pictures (radio) is generally considered superior to the media coverage with pictures (television). This may be true if you are blind or a bit dim, but it would be hard to justify by any other criterion. And yet we live in a country in which it is considered acceptable to say, 'I always turn down the sound on the television and listen to the radio instead.'

Let's say that again. Let's grasp the full stupidity of that single, bloodcurdlingly inane sentence. 'I always turn down the sound on the television and listen to the radio instead.'

Well, yes, we all said it when we were younger, because we thought it sounded impressive, in an iconoclastic, trend-hopping, unutterably pompous kind of way. Nowadays you have to wonder why anyone would wish to have the whole shooting match described for them in laborious radiophonic detail when over there, on the television, we can see what's happening for ourselves.

Test Match Special has its place, and that place is anywhere you can't watch the cricket on television. And yet the radio coverage is worshipped as a national institution, while the television coverage is patronised. When the BBC threatened to shove *Test Match Special* on to Radio 5 and dilute it with its redundant 'rolling-news' service, riots in the street were only narrowly averted. But when BBC Television broke off from the final overs of a fascinating Test against New Zealand for a first-round Wimbledon match featuring the newly waxed chest of André Agassi, only cricket fans objected.

Test Match Special's marginalisation of cricket is the secret of its immense popularity. When cricketing times are tough, as nowadays they always are, *TMS* operates as a sort of emotional buffer zone, inserting a nice cosy layer of sponge cake between us and the usual host of onfield disasters to stop us getting too upset about them. So what if England are 36 for 6? at least Blowers is on good form. This is why the death of Brian Johnston was mourned so keenly. Johnners, partly just by being called 'Johnners', had insulated us from cricketing failure for decades. With his loss, our defences were weakened, possibly irrevocably.

With the television coverage, there is no such buffer zone. It's all there in front of you. In June the dedicated couch potato might spend upwards of twelve full days peering at Richie Benaud's shock of white hair, or willing Geoffrey Boycott's straw hat to be blown off by the wind. There is no insulation from grim reality here. For the commentators do not distract you from England's failures; they emphasise them. 'Dear, oh dear, that were a terrible shot,' says Geoffrey. Pâtisserie has no place in this more rigorous environment.

We cannot love the television commentators as we love their radio counterparts. No one can form such an attachment to bearers of such consistently bad news. Indeed, as the rhythm of play swings against England once again, we start to hate the television commentators, despise and disdain their every uttering. Soon their every little quirk threatens to imperil the balance of our minds. Tom Graveney only had to say the words 'Really speaking . . .' for me to scream curses in five languages and propel innocent cushions in all directions. It wasn't his fault. He just didn't have anything to say, other than repeating what Richie had just said, with the addition of the words 'Really speaking' to add spurious authority to his pronouncements. If he had been on radio all those years, I doubt any of us would have been bothered.

Ray Illingworth's trick was to say everything twice. To say everything twice, that was Ray Illingworth's trick. Sometimes he used the same words, but in a different order. That's to say that the order was different, but the words were the same. Sometimes he used completely different words. The units of speech and writing, the very tools of language that he utilised were entirely dissimilar, not to mention utterly unalike. But the important thing was that, having said something, he then said it all over again. All over again, he said it, that was the important thing.

Nowadays we have Boycott and Bannister and David Gower and, of course, Richie Benaud, who is finally acknowledged as the doyen of commentators, now that all the other candidates have died. Survival is its own reward. Stay alive and you've got it made. Besides, only Benaud has ever had the temerity to look straight into the camera when being interviewed, in defiance of all television orthodoxy. When you are being interviewed, the rules state, you look at the interviewer, even if, offscreen, the interviewer is not looking at you. Benaud rejects such nonsense. Bypassing the interviewer and addressing the viewer direct is his unsubtle but effective method of taking complete control. Doyens don't need interviewers. Yes, go off and have a cup of tea, I'll look after everything here. Despite his increasing resemblance to the Yoda in *Star Wars*, you sense that no one mucks with Richie. You listen to what he says. Even Geoffrey Boycott occasionally listens to what he says.

Jim Laker was neither as versatile as Richie nor as articulate, and over the years he came to rely on a small repertoire of stock phrases for virtually every cricketing situation. But what a repertoire it was. Brief innings tended to be 'bright and breezy'. A well-timed shot was generally '4 from the moment it left the bat'. After it had passed the nearest fielder, you generally found that it was 'racin' away to the boundary'. When stumps were knocked clean out of the ground, the cry of 'And 'e's bowled 'im!' reverberated across the land. Laker's ultimate term of approbation was 'useful'. If a player completed 'a useful spell of bowlin'', he could have done no better. Laker's preoccupations, not least his almost infinite fascination with the life and works of Little Harry Pilling ('5ft 3 in his stockinged feet'), rubbed off on us all. At times he could be almost painfully prosaic. Not for Laker the wild poetic visions of an Arlott, or the wit and playfulness of a Johnston. But when England were doing well, I always wanted Laker to be commentating, because he could best communicate the wild emotions that underpin all great sporting achievements. At such moments intricate word paintings lost their appeal. What we wanted were big soppy outbursts of sentimentality, and Laker supplied them every time.

Best of all was the ineffable style with which he took the microphone for the very first ball of the day. After Peter West had greeted us, and disappeared to do whatever Peter Wests do all day, we invariably cut to the long-shot camera and, apparently, silence. The umpires were walking out, the crowd were taking their seats, but still . . . silence. Gradually the great man's wheezing would drift into earshot. Breathe in, breathe out, breathe in, breathe out – with just the faintest echo of phlegm in the lower register. You knew he was knackered. Those stairs had done him in again. After thirty seconds of the most laboured breathing you will ever hear outside a hospital ward, there came a huge intake of breath and, his strength finally restored, he uttered the first words of the day. 'Nkyou, Peter.' Then back to the heavy breathing. I waited ten years for the missing 'Tha', but it never quite squeezed out.

Richie's 'Thank you, Peters' never quite had the same weight, and I think it was when he realised this that he finally developed his own catchphrase, 'Morning, every-one'. But June will forever be marked as the month of the first Jim Laker impersonations. It is, I think, a fitting memorial.

Peter West disappeared some years ago to do whatever Peter Wests do in retirement, and in the absence of any more Peter Wests on the horizon, Tony Lewis is as sound a substitute as we could probably hope for. Many cricket fans object to his presence strongly because he is Welsh, although I think pity would be a more generous response than censure. If he looks a little nervous these days, it's probably because David Gower has recently joined the team and turned out to be an absolute natural: good-natured, intelligent, full of insights. For the moment, though, the commentator most under threat must be the dreaded Bannister. My attitudes here may be coloured by the Bannister's lengthy apologias for South Africa in the good old days before apartheid was abolished. No one argued more fervently than the Bannister for South Africa's speedy reintroduction into Test cricket, despite a handful of minor political problems that might have ensued as a consequence (such as the complete collapse of world sport). Then, when apartheid was finally dismantled, and South Africa were welcomed back, no one spoke more movingly than the Bannister of the wonders of multi-racial cricket – something that would have ceased altogether if he had had his way a few years earlier. The service in South African hotels isn't what it was, either, so I'm told.

These days the Bannister concentrates more on random attacks of meaningless hyperbole. Thus of Robin Smith, he says, 'There's no stronger hitter in world cricket.' Of Shane Warne, 'There's no bigger spinner of the ball in world cricket.' Of Allan Border, 'There's no cannier captain in world cricket.' It could be said, with some fairness, that there's no bigger talker of bollocks in world cricket.

Make yourself comfortable: it's going to be a long day. Mike Atherton has said that the three qualities required by the aspiring Test cricketer are talent, technique and temperament. They are, unsurprisingly, the same three qualities required by the aspiring Test viewer, for it takes guts to watch England's string of desperate failures without giving in to one's natural instinct to end it all and turn over to the schools programmes on BBC2. I was lucky. I was given a masterclass on the technique of Test viewing a decade or more ago, when my friend Richard came to stay for a few days at my parents' house. Before that weekend, I had been a dilettante. I had experienced frequent lapses in concentration, and had even been known to take phone calls while England were batting. But in his quiet, unobtrusive way, Richard showed me just what could be achieved with a little determination. At 10.50 on the first morning he placed himself in front of the television and sat still and silent for seven hours, anxiously chain-smoking. Not once did he pass comment. Not once did he rage at England's inadequacies. Lavatory breaks were timed to coincide with periods of inactivity, such as Mike Brearley's innings. Food was consumed rarely, and only in small, ascetic quantities. Nothing was allowed to disturb his concentration, although we went out for a drink every evening to discuss in eager detail the events of the day. In the end he sat like this for five full days without a single display of emotion. As it was the Headingley Test match of 1981, you can imagine how impressed I was.

Richard himself declines to explain his secret, although his recent tendency to call me Grasshopper and pretend he's Chinese may provide a few clues. But even a Zen master can crack sometimes. I have seen Richard crack only once – and he didn't so much crack as splinter into thousands of tiny lethal shards. Naturally, it wasn't cricket itself that generated this sudden outburst of fury. It was something far more disturbing: the absence of cricket.

This is one of the occupational hazards of serious cricket viewing. You forget that airtime is a precious commodity, and that in June, during what the *Radio Times* inevitably calls 'The Great British Summer of Sport', an awful lot of sporting events, each as vital and prestigious as the other, take place at exactly the same time.

So on a Saturday afternoon you settle down to watch the Test match on TV. The game is fascinatingly poised. The next hour could determine the course of the series. Whole careers are on the line. You have taken every reasonable precaution to ensure that you won't be interrupted (phone off hook, tinnies in fridge, door barricaded). Everything is set for an afternoon of the purest enjoyment.

And then Steve Rider pops up onscreen to say it's time for the 3.15 from Chepstow.

Er, what? Has there been some mistake? Does the cricket continue on BBC2? No, for on BBC2, one of Audie Murphy's more significant Westerns is being shown for the first time since a week last Wednesday. The cricket has vanished. Instead Julian Wilson is telling us that Intimate Deodorant is 7–2 favourite, while Colostomy Bag has dropped out of the running. 'It's a beautiful day here at Chepstow,' he fills in pathetically.

Shouting at the screen achieves nothing. Instead, we endure twenty minutes of undiluted equine agony, followed by a stewards' inquiry, a chat with the winning jockey, a chat with the winning jockey's mother and replays from thirty-seven different cameras. Then it's off to international croquet from Trondheim, where the plucky British team are flourishing in a commendable sixty-seventh place. By now you're desperate for a pee, but Ceefax tells you that 2 wickets have fallen, so you can't move in case Steve whisks us away from Norway back to the cricket action. What you don't know is that there is another race from Chepstow yet to come, followed by an unscheduled exclusive interview with Nick Faldo, by which time the batting side will be all out and your bladder will be the size of Swindon.

For Richard, the last straw is always Royal Ascot. England could be battling against the might of the Australians in a tussle of gladiatorial proportions, but we'd still be off every half-hour to Berkshire to watch middle-aged women in regrettable hats craning their papery necks to catch a glimpse of Princess Michael of Kent. Even Zen masters can't put up with that indefinitely. The mask cracks, and what he subsequently accuses Eve Pollard of doing with the winner of the 2.30 cannot be recorded here for obvious legal reasons.

When Richie does reappear, his sympathy is palpable. 'Welcome back,' he sighs, as if to say, 'It's all right! You can come out from behind the sofa! You're safe again!

We've got another eleven minutes of continuous coverage before the next interruption!'

And then, thirty seconds later, the rain starts and everyone sprints off the field, so after missing an hour of non-stop action, we can now watch commentators waffling for ten futile minutes before the programme moves, with some relief, to international table tennis from Düsseldorf. So much for the Great British Summer of Sport, and by corollary, the Great British Peace of Mind.

By mid-afternoon the spirit is as willing as ever, but the flesh is starting to weaken. Biscuit supplies are falling dangerously low, and the back-up packet of emergency Hobnobs may have to be called into action before the day is out. The harsh metallic aftertaste of stewed tea lingers in my mouth. I feel bloated because I haven't stopped eating. I feel hungry because what I have been eating has about as much nutritional value as a handful of soil. How much work could I have done in these wasted hours? Let's not even think about all the hundreds of thousands of hours previously wasted in exactly the same manner. I could have earned enough by now to be rampaging across the French Riviera in a gleaming new Porsche with a tanned large-breasted young lovely, while I anxiously twiddle the radio dial trying to pick up the cricket score on long wave . . . oh hell, oh blast.

If there is a general rule to be gleaned from this mess, it is that the more effort you put into watching cricket on television, the less cricket you will see. If it's not rain or bad light, it's Wimbledon or Royal Ascot – or it's the news every hour on the hour, and no matter if Graham Gooch is about to become the first Englishman to score 300 in a home Test in twenty-five years. Should you leave your television set for a moment, however, you will miss everything. Having watched every second of the 1994 series against South Africa, I walked out of the door minutes before DeFreitas and Gough started smashing the ball around at The Oval. The following day, while Malcolm was taking 9 wickets, I was in a traffic jam on the M40 on my way to a Scott match. You can't complain about it. These are the rules of the game.

Sometimes, by contrast, you just can't bear to watch. It's too painful. You have to get out of the house, do anything to distract yourself from the grim reality. I vividly remember passing Rumbelows in Camden Town in 1989, when England had to bat out the day to save the match in conditions which did not favour the bowlers. You would have bet on any team with a backbone to do it, which meant that, as usual, we were in real trouble. Shopping was the only alternative. But I had not bargained for Rumbelows. I tried not to look in the window, I really did. England were 134 for 4 and Robin Smith was taking guard at the crease, and I thought, 'Oh no, not again,' because it felt just like 1988 against the West Indies, and 1984 against the West Indies for that matter, and Smith was the last recognised batsman, and instantly he was out and it was 134 for 5 and I thought, 'I'm shopping! I'm shopping! Don't think about the cricket! Don't think about the cricket!' and I bought a sweater I have never worn since and a pair of shoes a size too small, which shows how effective that little mantra was.

The year before, during the calamitous West Indies series in which everyone captained England from Chris Cowdrey to Crystal Tipps and Alastair, I was in John Lewis with my girlfriend buying a telephone answering machine. We passed the television section, and I glanced at the screen, and the covers were being hauled on because England had just been all out for 93. The figure just sat there in the top right-hand corner. Ninety-three. I couldn't move. Three other men stood beside me, their mouths agape, each lost in his own private despair. We were the four brass monkeys: hear no evil, see no evil, bat no evil, bowl no evil.

The day finally stumbles to a close when Dickie Bird spots a tiny fluffy cloud edging in from Rochdale, and whips the players off for bad light. England are 110 for 4, or perhaps they lost the toss, in which case the opposition are 150 for 1. Strong team these days, Zimbabwe. I have put on two stone and contracted a number of diseases normally associated with malnutrition. We should never forget that Test cricket is a tough, remorseless game which takes no prisoners. It's probably not that easy to play, either.

CHAPTER TEN

The Bowlers

In village cricket, everyone is a bowler. No matter that only a tiny minority of players can actually bowl. What is important is that they all want to bowl, and they all think they can bowl. In particular, they all think that they can bowl better than the bloke who is bowling at the moment. How bizarre this notion is, and how cruelly self deluding. At more exalted levels of the game, bowlers are much-respected specialists who toil diligently at their craft in the modest hope of success and recognition. In Captain Scott, bowlers are everyone in the team besides me and Terence, and even Terence likes to turn his arm over from time to time. Talent doesn't come in to it. No, what counts is that if X has been given 6 overs, then Y feels aggrieved not to have had at least 7. So you give them 3 each, and make everyone unhappy.

All this hopeless manoeuvring is, however, good news for spectators, who in the course of a single village cricket match may watch fifteen or sixteen different trundlers plying their trade. Most of them are awful, of course, but awfulness boasts a diversity which mere excellence could never hope to emulate. There are only certain ways of bowling a good ball. Incompetence offers a far broader canvas. From the start of the bowler's run-up to the moment the batsman receives the ball on its fifth bounce, there is an almost infinite number of things that can go wrong. Some bowlers know what they are supposed to be doing, but can only do it some of the time. Others, to put it frankly, haven't a clue. It certainly makes captaincy interesting. With so many variables to be considered which could influence your bad bowler's performance, each bowling change becomes a giant leap into the unknown. Skill, temperament, form, confidence, yes, of course. But let's not forget large lunch, career uncertainties, bad trip on motorway, latent testosterone imbalance, presence of spectating girlfriend, unprescribed medication, paranoia, neurosis and sheer psychotic bloodymindedness, which alone has determined a few results. It's just as well there are so many bad batsmen about, or we'd really be in trouble.

With my friend Matthew, for instance, the crucial factor was a frighteningly low boredom threshold. As soon as his interest began to flag, after about his third ball, he would keep himself and everyone else amused by doing impersonations of celebrated 1970s bowlers. Curiously, the Bob Willis was the most accurate, but the Barry Wood took all the wickets. One day we were in the pub before a village game and someone said to us, 'You're the team with the Barry Wood bowler, aren't you?', remembering Matthew's feats of the previous year. His Bob Willises and Max Walkers were treated with disdain that afternoon, but they dead-batted every single Barry Wood.

Such multiplicity of bowling styles needs careful representation. To translate such infinite variety into a series of crudely drawn stereotypes would be misleading, and probably unfair. Still, why not? The bastards have never done me any favours.

Bowler 1: The Perennially Angry Fast Bowler

Of course we're not talking *fast*-fast here, for even our own Perennially Angry Fast Bowler, whom for reasons of discretion we shall call 'Tim', would be considered no more than military medium if let loose against proper batsmen. But Tim relies on more than mere speed, for, as team-mates and opponents can testify, he has a shorter fuse than Colonel Gadaffi. Ball hits pad. HOWZAT? Not out, says nervous umpire. Oh for *fuck's* sake, says Tim, wrenching his sweater from the umpire's grasp and removing most of the poor fellow's right arm in the process. I don't *fucking* believe it. Similarly, if someone drops a catch or misfields off his bowling, Tim struggles with his conscience for about 0.3 of a second – after all, he has dropped catches himself –

before letting fly with the sort of invective you would expect
to hear from someone whose dog you have just run over. If
umpires could send players off, Tim would be red-carded
every week.

The only response to such aggression is amused contempt. Nothing annoys Tim more than being laughed at.
We first encountered him when he was playing against
us for the *Financial Times*. He was even faster and more
ferocious in those days, but our opening batsmen that
day were uncharacteristically phlegmatic, and saw him
off. Later on he was judiciously murdered by Ian Wall
at his most formidable, and conceded 107 before he took
a wicket. Tim was boiling with rage. When he came out
to bat, he smote the ball with coruscating power – until
someone who was playing his first game for five years came
on to bowl. The first ball landed at the bowler's own feet,
where it stopped. Tim, eyes alight, bounded up the pitch
to hit it into a neighbouring borough. But the pitch was
situated on a steepish slope, and by the time he reached
the ball it was moving again, rolling down the middle of
the pitch directly towards his middle stump. Tim tried
every golf stroke in his repertoire, but he could not hit
it. To rousing laughter he was bowled. Francis Peckham,
our steely banker, was especially amused. Tim turned on
him. 'I suppose you think that's *fucking* funny, do you?'
he screamed. 'Yes I *fucking* do,' replied Francis, and the
two of them had to be prised apart before they killed
each other.

Later, after the match was over, Tim wandered up
to Harry and said, 'That was a jolly game, wasn't it?

Can I come and play for you?' He has never looked back.

Bowler 2: The Short-Arse

Beware the fast bowler of limited height. If ever there were someone with something to prove, it is he. Napoleon invaded Europe. A short fast bowler merely wants to send you to hospital. One of the nastiest I ever played against bowled 17 consecutive overs – all of them, luckily for him, downhill – on a pitch on which you wouldn't bet on Sunil Gavaskar to survive for long. It was a minefield. Balls leaped and kicked in every direction bar the one they would have taken on any normal pitch. But the bowler had no mercy. Years of aggravated shortness had obliterated every vestige of fellow feeling. Snarling with hatred at the long-legged majority, he made it clear from the first pad-busting missile that he was determined to get you out, but only if he couldn't kill you first. I made 1 run in 70 minutes. Bruises interlocked with bruises to form a lattice pattern of surprising subtlety: if I could have sold my thigh on the international art market I would have made a fortune. Every time I was knocked to the ground, he turned and walked back to his mark with a huge smirk on his tiny warped features. I survived more by incompetence than by judgement: the sheer slowness of my reactions helped me for the first time in my career. We learned later that he was a doctor. It's an area of

South Oxfordshire in which none of us ever intend
to fall ill.

Bowler 3: The Colonial Cousin

Cricketers are not racist, they just jump to conclusions
very easily. Therefore a long-limbed West Indian on the
other team (never 'black', always 'West Indian') will only
ever be a frighteningly swift fast bowler, equally adept at
ear-singeing bouncer and toe-crunching yorker. On the
village circuit of rural southern England, black players
are relatively rare, but when encountered, they spread
fear and trepidation amongst even the most confident
teams. Batsmen start strapping on extra protection, or
even asking to go a bit further down the order, give
someone else a chance, stomach feeling a bit dicky, sorry
Skip. Panic is not too strong a term. The possibility that a
black player may be as hopeless as the rest of us simply
never enters our minds.

But then English cricket, at every level, suffers from
a giant national (and racial) inferiority complex. Anyone darker or more Australian than the rest of us is
automatically assumed to be a superior cricketer. West
Indian bowlers are all Michael Holding, unless they have
a shortish run-up, in which case they're Malcolm Marshall.
Australians are all clean-hitting all-rounders with enormous
shoulders and boundless energy. For South Africans, see
Australians. Anyone originating from the Indian subcontinent is a wily spinner, capable of devilish turn and bounce

at will. If he can also do a reasonable impersonation of Abdul Qadir twirling the ball about before he comes in to bowl, he can psych out entire teams. Even New Zealanders are treated with exaggerated respect, just in case they turn out to be Sir Richard Hadlee.

None of them are ever that good, of course, but then they don't need to be – their mere presence does the job. Even after they have been rumbled, the subversion of the stereotype can still work in their favour. If the demon West Indian fast bowler turns out to be an off-spinner, for instance, the relief can erode a batsman's concentration to such an extent that he gets out to him in the softest manner possible. And yet the opposition are not the only people who can be fooled. The bowler's own captain can also assume too much. Possibly my best-ever innings was played against an Indian newsagent whose brother was rumoured to have played first-class cricket and who bowled luscious slow long hops conveniently wide of the off stump on a good pitch with a fast outfield on a warm day. I might have scored even more runs had tears of joy not restricted my vision. And yet his captain gave the newsagent 5 overs, which was approximately 4 overs more than he deserved.

Bowler 4: The Ex-Fast Bowler

In 1983, Martin D. was a fiery young pace bowler, tall and arrogant and bursting with youthful vim. Starting his run-up approximately 15 yards further back than he needed to, he would roar into the crease like a wronged rhino and unleash balls quick and short enough to put the wind up most student batsmen. There was little variety to his bowling: there didn't need to be. What counted was his snarling visage as he stormed past the umpire. Anguished grunts from the school of Monica Seles completed his repertoire. He was an impressive sight.

The first indication that things were beginning to go wrong came with the introduction of his first and so far only variation: the slower ball. Martin would still hurtle towards the crease making baboon noises, but instead of the customary snarl, a huge soupy grin was plastered over his taut features. The expected lollipop would then wobble harmlessly through the air, and the batsman would hit it for 4. Whatever else Martin had going for him as a bowler, a masterly exponent of guile he was not. Even Terence, who as a wicketkeeper has the reactions of a breezeblock, knew when the slower ball was coming.

At around the same time, Martin began to develop physically in a way in which naturally large and imposing figures tend to: outwards. His pace began to falter. Wickets became scarcer. The bowling average climbed. Soon every ball was as slow as the slower ball, and the slower ball barely moved at all.

This presented us with an interesting dilemma. Martin saw himself as a strike bowler. He didn't want to bowl first change, or learn new tricks. He just wanted to do a lot of snarling, and back that up with a bit of grunting. Aggression and raw pace were his trademarks, except without the raw pace. Opening batsmen were feeding on him with gluttonous relish. So, to motivate him a bit, we relegated him to first change. This made him angry enough to bowl quicker for a while, but by now there was no escape from the long-term effects of material success, happy marriage and bouncing children. Martin was mellowing. The snarls and outrage seemed more simulated than ever; a certain resignation now underpinned even his best efforts.

Martin D. is still playing regularly, and tends to bowl late in the innings against lower-order batsmen whom he routinely terrifies into surrendering their wickets. But his great days are over. He is a proud man who will never admit defeat. He needs your help. Send your cheque today.

Bowler 5: The Loose Popgun

Devon Malcolm is a loose cannon – magnificent one day, embarrassing the next. Our equivalent is Neal, the Loose Popgun. He is magnificent with one ball, and embarrassing with the next ten. He bowls slow wobbly little things of unpredictable length and line, happily conceding 30 runs in 4 overs. But in between the desperate wide long hops, the slow flaccid full tosses and the dismal leg-side half-volleys, you may well get two superb wicket-taking balls an over, swinging, dipping, bouncing and completely fooling the batsman. Whoa! What happened there? The problem is that Neal doesn't know either, as he simply bowls it and waits to see what happens. The Loose Popgun never has any idea what he is doing: it's just that, by some accident of nature, his body and his bowling action give him all the natural attributes any bowler could ever need. But the batsman can't believe this, and ties himself in knots trying to pick him. How can you predict someone's intent when he has no intent? After two consecutive jaffas, tiny bacteria of doubt start breeding inside the batsman's brain. Next is a facile full toss, which he pummels straight into mid-wicket's waiting hands. 'Lucky bastard,' breathe all the other bowlers. But he's not. He's one of the most dangerous bowlers in the team.

A word of caution, though. The Loose Popgun is only valuable if he maintains precisely the right level of incompetence throughout his career. One year, when we were very short of bowling, Neal bowled too often, and with practice he graduated from ineptitude to the murkier waters of mediocrity. Not only did he lose the bad balls, he lost the good balls as well. 4–0–30–4 became 4–2–12–0, which was no use to anyone. Now we bowl him rather more sparingly, and he's as bad as ever. Only one player in Scott history has taken more wickets.

Bowler 6: The Sensitive Flower

Pity the Sensitive Flower, for he cannot bear being hit for 4. It is the classic temperamental imbalance: the bowler who can be unplayable when everything is in his favour, but who collapses at the first sign of a counter-attack. Every team has at least one.

Again, it is often the most stroppy and arrogant players who suffer in this way. Furious, selfish and outspoken when thing are going well, the Sensitive Flower retreats into his own private purgatory after that first ball has gone sailing over his head for 4. He stumbles pathetically back to his mark, a broken man. He looks around for someone to blame. He can find no one. Each subsequent ball is about 5mph slower than the previous one. His shoulders slump. His head is bowed. You take him off at the end of the over.

Dealing with the Sensitive Flower can be one of the captain's most irksome tasks. One option is to bowl him early because opening batsmen rarely set out to destroy bowlers, and he might find a rhythm and do some damage. But his standard demeanour – sulky, indifferent, self righteous, bored – is sufficiently annoying that when he does start getting hit, you may feel that he deserves it. If you really are cruel you can keep him on for a couple more overs and see him creamed into oblivion. Soon he'll be begging to be taken off. 'I'm terribly short of bowlers today,' you lie. 'I'm relying on you to tie one end down.' You may lose the game, but everyone who has suffered the Sensitive Flower's moods will love you forever.

Bowler 7: Mr Corridor of Uncertainty

He was a good bowler once, got loads of wickets, and so he moved out of your orbit, moved up to better and finer teams, to play in leagues and perhaps even on the fringes of first-class cricket, and he practised, and he received careful coaching, and he learned the mystic secrets of length and line, and he pitched it up and swung it late, and always bowled in the corridor of uncertainty, and the batsman had to play at it – *click* – and there it went, into the safe hands of third slip, and he did well.

And then he came back to play in your team for a day, when you needed someone really good to beat a side you really hate, and he bowled in the corridor of uncertainty, every ball, what a beautiful length, and the batsmen weren't good enough to hit it, or they slogged him over the slips, or they nicked it and because your team can't field, the slips couldn't catch a thing, and he took 0–45 in 10 overs.

Bowler 8: The Donkey-Dropper

Introduce a little humour into a cricket match and the immediate victim is dignity. Donkey-drop bowlers present a unique threat to a batsman – the threat of humiliation. Everybody else smiles as the Donkey-Dropper is given the ball, as they all know how bad he is. If he gets a wicket, the fielders' first reaction will be to laugh. Ostensibly, he is the captain's greatest gamble. In fact, if deployed at the right moment, he is an entirely risk-free investment. The worst that can happen is what you expect will happen: 1–0–26–0. The best is that some sorry batsman may get out to him.

There are essentially two sorts of Donkey-Droppers: those who do it on purpose and those who don't. The ones who do it on purpose tend to be brought on late in the summer, late in the afternoon, when the sun is high behind the bowler's arm. How very naughty. We have found that when teams do this to us, it's entirely by mistake, whereas when we do it to them, we are cheating. Good grief, how could they think that? What sort of people do they think we are?

Donkey-Dropper type 2 is best represented by Terence, who simply doesn't know how to bowl. He imparts no spin to the ball; indeed he barely imparts the ball itself, so slowly does it emerge from his hand. The arc is magnificent, as is the violence with which the batsman customarily greets it. Even Terence, though, has had his moments. Indeed, it was he who bowled the best ball I have ever seen. As ever it flew high in the air, but it was of a fuller length than usual, and it became clear, as we all watched its trajectory, that this ball was predestined to drop directly on top of middle stump. The batsman realised this too, and was in at least four minds about how to deal with it. In the end he tried a sort of crazed reverse sweep over the stumps, and was lucky enough to edge it, diverting the ball down in front of the stumps, where it hit the batsman's mark, and bounced straight back to hit middle and off. Even Shane Warne couldn't manage that.

Bowler 9: Unlucky

'Ooh! Unlucky!' the fielders cry. The Unlucky Bowler plugs away, every ball on the spot, forcing the batsman to play, not conceding any runs, not taking any wickets.

This is a dreadful fate for any bowler. You bowl to take wickets, not to concede 2 runs an over and watch Arvind clean up at the other end. But this is the fate of a thousand Unlucky Bowlers, doomed to look good and achieve little. Our own, who has long laboured under the ominously unfortunate nickname of Gags, bowls left-arm over the wicket and says faintly aggressive things like 'I'll take him', but we all know he won't. He is so unlucky that his stock ball is the inswinger, a ball left-armers usually find hard to bowl, but not Gags, even though an outswinger would be rather more helpful. 'I'll mix it up a bit,' he says, before bowling exactly the same ball he always bowls. After an over or so working him out, the batsmen will start popping him behind square leg for a single or, if his length varies at all, carting him over mid-wicket for 4. Meanwhile, at the other end, Arvind has so far taken 4 wickets. 'I'm softening them up for him,' says Gags, not untruthfully. But that's not the way it looks in the scorebook. Six overs, no maidens, 15 runs, no wickets . . .

Bowler 10: *The Useless Stranger*

One of the regulars brings him along. He tells you he can bowl a bit, smiling modestly as if to say, 'Hey, I'm too cool to oversell myself but let's face it, I'm probably too cool to play for this team anyway.' Or he is too shy and intense to look you in the eye and tells his shoes that he can bowl a bit, with that tinge of aggression that says, 'If I had a few social graces, I'd be playing first-class cricket by now.' Or he says he used to bowl a bit at school, or at college, or for his for county's Under-19s (a surprisingly common lie). And the regular player, his sponsor, comes over later to have a quiet word. 'I haven't seen him bowl myself, but I've heard good things about him.' Yes, I'm sure you have.

Because every time, like a mug, you give the newcomer 3 or 4 overs – you might even bowl him first change. And he is terrible. Confident, keen, determined, but terrible. 'Haven't quite got my spinning finger going yet, Skip.' What? It hasn't been amputated? 'Bit short of practice, Skip.' Twenty years' unbroken practice against five-year-old girls who had never picked up a bat in their lives and he still wouldn't get a wicket. 'Problems with the grip, Skip.' You imagine gripping him by the neck, squeezing the last breath from his malformed frame. But one of the regulars has brought him along, probably as a favour because you were a player short, so you have to be polite. Then the batsman hits an innocuous full toss straight at a fielder, who drops it, and the Useless Stranger throws a huge petulant tantrum. Hmm, you think, maybe this fellow will fit into the team after all.

Bowler 11: Mr Try Anything Once

The obverse of the unlucky bowler, Mr Try Anything Once does not believe in the idea of the 'stock ball'. Everything is different; nothing is what it's supposed to be. Leg-breaks mix with off-breaks and googlies and flippers and fast straight ones and all sorts of esoteric experiments, each bowled with a huge mischievous grin, as if to say to the batsman, 'Guess what I've got up my sleeve now.'

Unfortunately, the batsman knows exactly what he's got up his sleeve – a slow full toss. For Mr Try Anything Once's experiments would be much more effective if he could get any of them to land. Of the few that do encounter the pitch on the way to the meat of the bat, most bounce at least twice, although with Mr Try Anything Once, it is possible that that is another of his ingenious variations. Once every other over, he bowls a beautiful fizzing leg-break of perfect length and line that befuddles the batsman and, half a second later, the wicketkeeper, before making straight for the boundary and 4 byes. But he never gives up, He is, after all, Mr Try Anything Once.

Bowler 12: The Enigma

Only the Enigma knows. Sometimes it works, sometimes it doesn't. But only the Enigma knows. And he is saying nothing. So everyone waits. And he bowls. And the batsman clips him high over deep mid-wicket for 6. It's not working today. Damn.

CHAPTER ELEVEN

July: Chariots of Fire

You might ask where one finds time in all this for relationships, and in July you get the answer. She leaves you. She has had enough. If it were just cricket on Sunday, well, she could understand that. She could even take the odd game on Saturday if there was nothing else on. But when you add up all the midweek games, the days in front of the Test match on television, your unhealthy devotion to your cricket pads and your unfortunate tendency to shout 'No-ball!' at the moment of orgasm, you can see she has a point. I was planning to call this chapter 'Cricket and Sex' but, as all cricketers know, the two rarely mix. The rumour persists that cricketers are, in some wholesome way, more attractive to women than most sportsmen – but

that's all it is, a rumour, put about to console us for our
failure to hold down any sort of sensible relationship for
longer than a Sussex first innings. In reality the white of
our trousers represents more than our regular use of Persil
Power to get out those nasty grass stains. Or do you prefer
Ariel Automatic? In Captain Scott these days we talk of
little else.

You can sense the team's crippling disappointment. In
adolescence, we all noticed the girls flocking around the
First XI, and at that moment the game's appeal suddenly
magnified and, in some cases, throbbed painfully. Even
when blinded by the hormonal maelstrom of our youth,
we knew that the male physique was flattered by cricket
whites. The only problem was that, at the time, none of
us really had a physique to flatter. But the seed had been
planted. Cricket was sexy, and if we practised our forward
defensives long enough, maybe we could be too.

In particular, girls seemed fascinated by the way bowlers
rubbed the ball in their groins. You may wonder – as I
always have – why this particular region of the body was
selected as the most convenient place to shine a cricket
ball. But the girls knew. One girl I was keen on could
watch it on television for hours. Rub rub rub rub rub. I
tried everything to distract her, but to no avail. Later on
we started Captain Scott, at least partly in the hope that
marauding gangs of sex-starved young undergraduettes
would assault us after each game in a frenzy of carnal
anticipation. Unless you count the unwanted attentions of
a slightly excitable labrador at one game in 1981, nothing
of the sort ever happened. Somehow we had missed the

boat, or missed the point. We had certainly missed the marauding gangs of sex-starved undergraduettes.

Indeed, about the first display of interest came in our sixth season, when a small group of girlfriends rather tentatively accompanied us to a match in Cambridge. Did we think we were cool? We did. The word groupies was even bandied about, a little recklessly, as it happened. For what we didn't know was that, fuelled by boredom and a few large gins at lunchtime, the women were ruthlessly assessing each member of the team in his capacity as sex object. Not a single hold was barred or blush spared in this comprehensive and outspoken appraisal. And the chances are that none of us would ever have known a thing about it, had I not happened to catch them in mid-discussion. What was shocking, though, was that their judgements were far from complimentary. Indeed, most of us were damned as 'much of a muchness'. The team was dumbfounded. Much of a muchness? Were our finely wrought bodies, carved by the hand of God from the essence of life itself, not exemplary specimens of glowing manhood at its most vibrant and athletic? No, they weren't. They were much of a muchness.

Only two players were excepted from this blanket condemnation. Bill Hoath, then our regular wicketkeeper, was unanimously voted Mr Captain Scott Invitation XI 1984. The judges, in their summing up, spoke of his 'clean-cut demeanour', which, to one observer, explicitly recalled the film *Chariots of Fire*. From then on, with typical subtlety, the player in question was forever known as Bill 'Chariots of Fire' Hoath, and became our official team sex symbol.

The only other player to be singled out by the panel was deemed to have a face like a squished tomato. This caused much amusement, but it also put an end to our dreams of being worshipped as demigods.

What became clear is that women adore men in cricket whites as long as they look pretty good to start off with. The attractions of Imran Khan, for instance, are well documented. As far as men are concerned, he was Pakistan's best captain in living memory, a fine free-flowing batsman and a magnificent fast bowler with a vicious inswinging yorker. For the female viewpoint I conducted an informal telephone poll amongst some of my women friends, who, after short pauses to get their breath back, declared him 'hot', 'horny' and 'a babe'. Some slight divergence there on sexual grounds, I think.

Equally telling scenes have taken place at Scott games whenever a certain floppy-haired English actor, now globally famous, has made one of his occasional appearances for the team. Before his breakthrough film, wives and girlfriends merely asked to be informed whenever he was playing as it would probably be a splendid day for a picnic. They would sit to one side and coo softly whenever he flopped his hair back or looked particularly adorable. He would charm their socks off and then go and talk football with the blokes. Since megastardom struck, however, his life has become more complicated. Indeed, he has played for us only once, and on that occasion found himself mobbed by a gang of teenage lovelies, who used the excuse of autograph-hunting to indulge in rudimentary frottage. The rest of the team could do nothing but stand by and observe the madness, and throw the occasional bucket of water over their own drooling wives. To be in the presence of such an icon of male perfection in such circumstances is to find yourself magically transformed into the Elephant Man.

Even if there are no film stars in your team, cricket can place unusual strains on a relationship. The tendency of men to compartmentalise their lives finds no more pertinent illustration than their defensive posturing on the matter of cricket. You meet someone, you fall in love, and you introduce her to your friends and parents. She introduces you to her friends and parents, and that goes all right, so you set up home together and haunt DIY shops on late-opening Thursdays and hold dinner parties in which you try to pair off single people who would rather eat raw sewage than be paired off with each other. These are the normal rhythms of life. But still you haven't shown her what you do on Sundays. Off you trot at 11.30 with a bag full of foul-smelling cricket equipment – which, being a 1990s sort of guy, you have insisted on washing yourself, only you haven't quite got round to it yet – and back you slink at 8.30, tired, sweaty and disillusioned, with a huge purple mark on your thigh and a serious groin strain. Well, I don't know about you, but in her place I would get suspicious. Sooner or later, she will want to come along and see what you get up to. She will want to watch. You. Playing cricket. Very badly.

Being sensible, you will want to delay this moment for as long as possible. The relationship is working so well, so why ruin it? Love is founded on mutual respect. Respect is inextricably tied up with pride and dignity. But there is nothing terribly dignified about playing village cricket. And there will be nothing remotely dignified about the way you play it when the woman of your dreams is sitting on the sidelines willing you to do something she can be impressed by. On the only occasion one particular girlfriend came to see me play (in four years), I didn't bowl, I didn't bat, and I dropped an easy catch. 'But what did you do?' she asked later. Well, I was captaining, I said. 'So why didn't you make sure you bowled or batted?' She didn't even refer to the pathetic dropped catch. After that things were never quite the same again.

It's even worse with parents. Ian Wall is a big, aggressive, imposing bloke in whose giant hands a mere bat looks puny and insignificant. He carts bowling of all types to all areas of the ground. Then his father comes to watch a game and Ian shuffles out to the crease like a condemned man. One ball later he's on his way back, head down and ready for the barrage of amused abuse his father will hand out. It doesn't matter that Ian's dad is just as keen as Ian that he should do well. It is just inevitable that he won't.

Fortunately, no girlfriend of mine ever played for the Cheshire League. But taking anyone to a cricket match is just asking for trouble. What will she think of your team-mates? What will they think of her? One thing that needs explaining – preferably in the car on the way up – is that just because you play sport with people it doesn't necessarily follow that you like them that much. They're just your 'sports friends'. This isn't strictly true, but it may well help you later when Tim starts chasing someone around with a raised stump, or Arvind tries to sell your girlfriend some shares in a supermarket chain.

Then there are the wives. Cricket wives are the survivors. For years they have tolerated their pathetic husbands' unquenchable desire to run stoutly around remote cricket pitches pretending that adulthood never happened. In the eyes of every cricket wife lies an unasked question – 'Did I marry him for this?' – the answer to which is no. At one time they probably harboured hopes of weaning their idiot spouses from this stupid sport, for every cricket wife knows an ex-cricket wife who has managed the transition painlessly. The trouble is, every cricket wife also knows a cricket ex-wife who wasn't so successful. The cricket wives have chosen the middle way – at least for now. The war isn't over, but a ceasefire has been declared. Lull the poor fool into a false sense of security. He thinks he's won. Just wait.

Actually, in Captain Scott, all the wives have become great friends and bring their children to matches, and now the children are becoming great friends – and if this sounds suspiciously like an episode of *The Waltons*, then I would have to admit that the happy families atmosphere we enjoy at certain games is far from unpleasant. All the children are of an age at which they need constant attention, and what could be safer than a village cricket pitch in the middle of rural England? Parents can take it in turns to keep the children in line, allowing all the others to drift into mid-afternoon reveries or read improving volumes (the *News of the World*). Other than the huge driven 6s that generally result from the introduction into the attack of one of our spin-bowlers, there is no danger to the little ones at all.

Even so, it can be an intimidating experience for any newcomer to enter this cosy domestic scene – especially if you have forgotten to bring a tartan picnic blanket for her. This is very much your responsibility: a tartan picnic blanket not only prevents pneumonia but allows your girlfriend to keep clear of the other spectators should she fail to find them suitably gripping company. Similarly, you must be equipped with at least two thick sweaters to lend her when it gets cold, and enough Sunday newspapers to wallpaper a ballroom. You know how bored she is going to be, even if she doesn't, and you must be prepared.

It is when you are out on the field that your paranoia reaches its apogee. Your girlfriend may not hit it off with the cricket wives, or worse, she may hit it off with them too well. What if they are having the 'Don't-make-the-same-mistake-I-made' conversation? Or the 'Christ-he's-a-loser-what-on-earth-do-you-see-in-him' conversation? Such mindless speculations make it difficult to concentrate on the game. One of our more mercurial batsmen hit upon a rich seam of form a couple of years ago while in the throes of a painful divorce, and one day scored a sparkling 83 not out. Aha, he thought, a splendid way to impress the lovelies. So, for the next few weeks, he brought along a string of women to cricket matches, and was out for 0 every time. One day the woman was late, and he scored 46; minutes before she turned up, he was out. Eventually he met and fell in love with a woman whom he has since married – but was lucky enough to do so in November, long after the end of the season. The fact that they are visibly perfect for each other is incidental. If they had met in June, how long would the relationship have survived?

Cricket wives should not be confused here with cricket widows, whose attitude towards the game tends to be less yielding. Cricket widows have decided to just ignore the whole sorry business in the hope that eventually it will go away. I myself remain unconvinced that this tactic works, but when emotional wars this fierce are being fought, you can't really blame anyone for doing what she thinks is right. One cricket widow, while in her cups, recently told me that she wished her husband was doing something a little less sad with his weekends, 'like having an affair'. Some cricket widows, though, try too hard to wean their partners away from the game they love. This can be terribly risky. One friend of mine was actually given the great cricketing ultimatum – 'It's cricket or me.' My friend thought about this for a second, and chose cricket. She must have known he would. If Cindy Crawford had given him the ultimatum, his decision would probably have been the same. In the end, my friend and his beloved sorted out their differences and were later married, but that simple choice, 'It's cricket or me,' erased nearly two years from their relationship. He's still playing, of course.

What none of this involves, of course, is sex. That cricket is profoundly unsexy was discovered the hard way by the scorer of 83 not out to whom I referred earlier (you will have noticed that I am being a little less free with the Christian names in this chapter), but at heart I think we all know it to be true. When another player was spotted

in the changing room with massive scratches all over his
back, we all made the required jokes about his sex life, but
I doubt that it occurred to any of us that he had one. If he
had said that he had been mauled by an escaped panther,
we would probably all have believed him.

And now that Imran Khan has retired, first-class cricket
is painfully short of internationally acknowledged sex sym-
bols. Mike Gatting's barmaid experience was so shocking
because it had never occurred to us that anyone could con-
ceivably find Mike Gatting attractive. Another telephone
poll of my female friends revealed that none of them would
be prepared to sleep with Ian Botham for less than £85,000.
(Others wanted much more, but one was particularly keen
to pay off her mortgage.)

A partial explanation may be that for as long as anyone
can remember, England players have all had very large
bottoms. From Tom Graveney and Colin Cowdrey, through
Gooch and Lamb to the sizeable packet now boasted by
Angus Fraser, our Test cricketers have consistently been
well endowed in the posterior department. Mike Gatting
has a whopper. Ian Botham's is about as big a bottom as
you can get without falling over.

Purely in terms of Test selection, this is surely no
coincidence. How did Allan Lamb play 75 Tests at an
average in the mid-thirties while Derek Randall played
only 47 and was usually put in to open because no
one else wanted to go there? Because Randall had no
buttocks at all to speak of, while Lamb, though born and
bred in South Africa, was about as English as they come
in all matters bottom-related. Why did Phil Edmonds play

so many fewer Tests than his Middlesex 'spin-twin' John Emburey? Because Emburey was a much better bowler? Because Edmonds didn't 'get on' with Mike Brearley? Look at their trouser padding before you come to any conclusions.

Doubtless there are good tactical reasons for this preferential treatment – think how rarely Colin Cowdrey was bowled around his legs – but it hardly improves cricket's image. It is well documented that women prefer men with small, pert, shapely bottoms, so when they see Graham Gooch lumbering around the outfield, his cheeks wobbling behind him, their reaction is naturally one of disgust. It is curious that small-bottomed cricketers like David Gower have never really been accepted by the large-trousered hegemony. Perhaps they are thought to have insufficient gravitas.

Even if the bottoms don't get you, the voices will. Imran Khan, as well as all his other attributes, has a deep dark brown voice, proud and aristocratic. Compare, if you will, Graham Gooch's Essex squeak, or Mike Gatting's uncanny Alan Ball impersonation.

Cricket and sex, therefore, are mutually exclusive, even if you do remember to wear a box. About the only cricketers who do get anywhere, it seems, are women cricketers, but only (according to a friend of mine who has played women's cricket for some years) with each other. Apparently the make-up of some teams is constantly changing, because if A has had an affair with B, but is now going out with C, then C won't wish to play in the same team as B, especially as she is now involved with C's old flame D. Meanwhile E has gone off to play with F's team, who are desperate for new players after it was revealed that G had been sleeping with H, J, K and L. Few of us can have encountered anything similar in the male game: in fact, compared to the same-sexing hotbed that is Association Football, cricket seems to hold few attractions for gay men. Perhaps the bottoms put them off as well.

You might then ask what cricketers do in bed, and the straightforward answer is: sleep. One Scott stalwart, whom we shall rename for the purposes of this chapter Mr Sad, occasionally uses his eight hours to 'soften up' items of brand-new kit for the following weekend's games. It is a procedure, he assures me, that has many adherents in the cricketing world, but I'd be intrigued to find out what their wives think about it. There they lie, fast asleep, dreaming of dark, handsome men with deep blue eyes who say impossibly romantic things like 'Cricket? No, never played it in my life,' when suddenly they are awakened by a stray wicketkeeping glove. The pads, says Mr Sad, particularly benefit from such treatment, although I do feel honour-bound to point out that he and his longtime girlfriend have yet to have any children. Condoms break, and you can always forget to take the pill, but cricket pads never let you down.

The irony is that cricketers should be rather good at it. Fast bowlers may be at something of a disadvantage, but wrist-spinners should have a great time, and in an ideal world, finger-spinners would be at a premium. But there can be nothing gained from dwelling on what might have been. Take the example of Bill 'Chariots of Fire' Hoath.

Not long after his rechristening, he found a girlfriend who didn't like cricket, moved in with her, married her and then, by letter, retired from cricket forever. None of us have ever seen him since. The pressure of being our official sex symbol, with the burden of a thousand women's dreams weighing on his shoulders, had just been too much for him. Remember Colin Welland picking up the Oscar for *Chariots of Fire* and shouting, 'The British are coming'? He was wrong then, and he's wrong now.

CHAPTER TWELVE

Ground-to-Air Missiles

England team managers on tour have three important tasks: carry the bags, organise fielding practice, take the blame. In a Captain Scott season, the bags are carried by anyone unlucky enough to be passing Harry's car when he unlocks the boot. The blame is shared fairly between all members of the team, unless the captain is out of earshot, in which case it's all his fault. As for fielding practice – well, what a marvellous idea. We must try it some day.

In village cricket no one thinks about fielding until it's too late. Most of us work at our batting, and one or two bowlers even accept the need for an occasional net. Yet the nearest most teams get to a fielding practice is a desultory game of catch just before each game gets underway. The first four or five people out of the changing room jog aimlessly on to the outfield and look for something to do. Someone grabs a ball. The four or five arrange themselves into an approximate circle and throw the ball at each other. The show-offs throw it high in the air for other people to drop. The players who can't throw for toffee stand a little closer to the centre of the circle so they won't be made to look stupid. Eventually someone throws the ball too far and fast, one person runs off to recover it, and everyone else wanders back to the pavilion for another cigarette. End of fielding practice.

And yet the same people will sit in the pub a few hours later and pompously take the England team to task for its rather stately fielding. 'Catches win matches,' someone will say, to widespread groans. How many catches did we drop today? How many hopeless misfields were there? Just don't ask.

The truth is we can't be bothered. It's too much of an effort. If cricket were a true team game, we would feel honour-bound to support the brave efforts of our bowling comrades with appropriately energetic and committed performances in the field. But it isn't and we don't. Fielding is the price you pay for batting and bowling, unless you are Jonty Rhodes, and not many of us are. We could all improve, of course, but we would have to work at it. What a grim thought. There is no point in compromising, so many village players take the opposite route: complete idleness. We languish. We stonedrift. We field more like Cecil Rhodes than Jonty.

But we still appreciate excellence when we see it. When

Cliff isn't running out his fellow batsmen, it is pure pleasure to watch him trying to run out some of the opposition's. In he swoops, and before your eyes have had time to adjust, the ball is in the 'keeper's hands over the stumps. I sometimes think I would have as much chance of running someone out if I posted the bloody ball first class.

Cliff catches superbly as well: infield, outfield, fast, slow, high, low. When he leaps like a salmon to take a catch at extra cover, we roar with joy and triumph. Most of us can leap no higher than smoked salmon, so Cliff's displays of athleticism seem almost supernatural. You tend to wonder where he has hidden the ladder.

The performances of the other fielders in Scott vary enormously, for all are capable of crass misjudgements as well as occasional moments of brilliance. Our floppy-haired actor, for instance, doesn't look anything out of the ordinary but has an amazing knack for taking catches. This may have a lot to do with being in the right place at the right time, which is in itself a rare and beautiful talent much undervalued by an envious world.

A rarer and more tragic case is the good ground-fielder who cannot take catches. My old friend Patrick, who captained the team for a couple of years in the mid-1980s, suffered from this. No one could have been more reliable when retrieving the ball, or even carrying off the odd diving stop to prevent a certain boundary. But hit the ball in the air at him and he hadn't a chance. It was the split-second he had to think about it that made all the difference. He wasn't scared of the ball; he was scared of dropping the ball, and looking a fool. It was an important difference, although it made no difference to anyone watching. To them he looked like a fool who was scared of the ball.

Then there are the oddities. One regular, who is prone to glooms, cannot run any faster than walking pace. He has a perfectly safe pair of hands, and can throw well, but his steps are so small that he looks like one of those speeded-up characters who used to chase each other around in Benny Hill sketches. So as he pursues the departing ball, we all sing the Benny Hill theme tune to give him some encouragement. It doesn't work, but it cheers us up.

Many fielders suffer from fear of the ball, and the weird thing about this is the way it gets worse as you get older. I know at least one person who has stopped playing because of it; and after dislocating my finger while dropping a catch a couple of years ago, I feel appreciably less confident about my own fielding. One particular solicitor from Delhi, however, has a terror of the speeding ball that verges on the pathological. If anyone whacks it in his general direction, his instinct – and one cannot entirely blame him for this – is to get the fuck out of the way. It is worth noting, however, that huge yellow feathers only grow out of his back when he is fielding to someone else's bowling. When he himself is bowling, he is fearless. Gordon Banks would not have disowned some of his saves.

To be fair, though, one could say the same of virtually anyone who bowls at this level. A bowler, to save just one run, will fling himself upon a speeding ball as though dodging a bullet. Caught and bowleds are rarely less than spectacular. Next over the bowler is down at long leg doing his celebrated impersonation of fotherington tomas ('Hello clouds, hello sky') and a comfortable catch flies past his head for a one-bounce 4. It is amazing what a difference it can make when your own bowling figures are the ones at risk.

Down and down the evolutionary ladder we go. Below Cliff and Bill and Arvind and the floppy-haired megastar, below even the final rung, down there in the primeval slime, swim the cricketing plankton – me, Terence and Stephen. We try our best. Sometimes we try so hard it's painful. But the three of us, and a couple of others, have one fundamental flaw in our technique: we throw like girls. How marvellous it would be to whip the ball in over the stumps from 60 yards with a single flick of the wrist. But no: we shot-putt the ball pathetically into the air and if it goes 20 feet spectators break out into spontaneous applause. Terence has developed an ingenious method of avoiding this weekly humiliation: he keeps wicket. If for some reason he is denied this safe haven, he always throws the ball in underarm, citing a dicky shoulder. Strangely, Stephen and I have also recently developed long-term shoulder injuries, and rub our upper arms dramatically whenever anyone raises a sceptical eyebrow. Occasionally, though, circumstances dictate that we have to fling the ball in at high speed, perhaps when Richard has yelled: 'Keep the batsman down to five.' Because we are so out of practice, we really do put our shoulders out, and wander around in agony, ignored by scornful team-mates.

Sometimes we try so hard it's painful. In 1985 Captain Scott enjoyed a tough match at Tilford in Surrey, which boiled down, after hours of diligent effort on both sides, to a simple equation: one ball left, Tilford 2 short of our total. As it was an overs match, we didn't need to get them out. If the batsman scored only 1 run, we won. If he scored 2, it was a tie. If he scored 3, we lost. All very straightforward. We all knew what was required. The bowler ran in to bowl the final ball.

The batsman decided to go for the big one. Amazingly, he connected. Even more amazingly, Terence, at silly mid-off, fielded it cleanly. The batsman called yes and charged up the field.

All Terence had to do now was wander nonchalantly to the stumps and knock them over. Instead he panicked, and tried to throw the stumps down. He missed by miles. The ball flew down to long leg. Stephen ran round from square leg to fetch it. By now the batsmen were coming back for a second run. Stephen panicked as well. In attempting to return the ball to the wicketkeeper, he somehow managed to lollop it over to third man. There was no third man. Bill 'Chariots of Fire' Hoath, the 'keeper, had to run down to collect it himself. By the time he had thrown it in, the batsmen had scored the three runs they needed and won the game.

It was a famous defeat. Many of our team were furious. As far as they were concerned, Terence's and Stephen's mucking about had cost us a deserved victory. In fact the reverse was true. Stephen and Terence had tried as hard as they physically could, and, in doing so, had scaled levels of incompetence of which probably even they had not thought themselves capable. There is victory in every defeat, if you look close enough for it. In this instance, I am not sure we could have looked much closer.

Most of the time, though, the three of us can get by without humiliating ourselves or the team (Tilford never played us again). It is a matter of camouflage. The highest priority for a pitiful fielder is not to be found out. If you can reach the end of a fielding innings without the other team taking a single to you every ball, I think you can regard that as a result. Any idiot can show how good he is, but to conceal ineptitude is a real art. Pay attention there at the back.

First, make sure that you are fielding close to the wicket: cover point, square leg, mid-wicket, mid-on. Mid-off is more dangerous, as for the other bowler you may be forced to field at deep backward square, where you will certainly be found out. Remember your dicky shoulder – rub it frequently, and before the game ask if anyone has any Deep Heat spray as it's playing up a bit today. You have to field close in, and can only throw underarm, but you will feint the quick whipped-in throw every time the batsman wanders out of his crease on the off-chance. Right, that's your captain fooled. Now for the opposition. Remember to walk in before every ball. Only the best and worst fielders on a team walk in – the best because they are genuinely enthusiastic and the worst because they want everyone to think they are the best. Look keen. Show off a bit, especially when it doesn't matter. A well-timed dive can only be to your credit, whether or not you had the slightest chance of reaching the ball. It also saves you having to run back and get it. Always back up. It's easy, and anyone who stops the ball backing up is invariably a hero, if only because some other idiot failed to do it ten minutes ago and the ball went for four overthrows. If, by some miracle, you do something impressive, stay cool about it. Everyone should think you're always as good as that.

Make sure the ball comes to you on its way back to the bowler. This is a good opportunity to experiment with different ways of catching the ball: hands up like the Australians, hand down like the British, or hands flapping from side to side like the sea lions at London Zoo. Keep your mouth shut as the ball loops through the air. Do not hyperventilate, or cry. And do not put your hands in the air until a split-second before you catch the ball: this looks cool, and it doesn't matter if you drop it, because it is better to look as though you are going to catch it than actually to catch it. When you have picked up the ball, study it with care. Polish it. Always keep hold of it half a second too long. This helps foster the impression that you have been fielding the ball constantly, whether you have or not.

Close fielding is a different matter, especially if you are keen on staying alive. A bad fielder will be found out quickly at short leg, for the ball will be off on its travels some seconds before you leap screaming out of the way. You don't have the reactions to avoid it, let alone catch it, and you are terrified anyway, so if asked to field there, develop a sudden eye problem and tell the captain you have left your drops in the car. Slip is easier because no one takes any catches there in any case, and it may as well be you not catching them as anyone else. Besides, if by chance you do take one, you will be a hero. Leg slip is subtle but dangerous. Avoid it unless you don't mind complex bone fractures.

Of course, it does help if the captain puts you in the right place. Should I be here at square leg, or would I be better off just behind square? Over at mid-off, the captain is also wondering about this. Should he be at square leg, or should I put someone there who can field?

But the greatest challenge to any fielder is to stay awake. On a lazy summer Sunday afternoon, down at third man, forty minutes before tea, with the sun caressing your eyelids and songbirds warbling over the ambient drone of the new bypass, when you haven't fielded the ball for nearly half an hour, and the lunchtime lager has dulled the few senses you have left over after a long week, you can't be blamed for losing the plot a little. Dr Hannibal Lecter would have trouble concentrating in such circumstances. So you drift off into a blissful reverie where you feel at one with nature. Time slows to a standstill. Nothing seems to matter. Everything seems so vivid – the smell of newly mown grass, the variegated greens of the massed foliage, the sounds of local adolescents copulating in the bushes.

And someone, somewhere in the distance, shouting 'Catch!' Oh, my God . . .

CHAPTER THIRTEEN

July: A Day Out

To the Test match with my friend Andy Robson. Andy
is a cricketer too, but a real cricketer, who plays in
a real league team, and can really bat and bowl. He
played for Captain Scott once, and although he took
no wickets and scored only 4, he did throw down the
stumps from deep third man, which alone justified the
reputation I had been so busy inflating on his behalf
for most of the previous week. He doesn't even have the
excuse of youth for such wanton displays of excellence.
Andy is staring forty down the barrel, and spends his
weekends captaining a side whose players are half his
age or under. We don't talk cricket often, but once
we get started we can go on all day. He is the perfect

companion for seven hours of gloom at the cradle of cricket.

It is a couple of years since I have been to a Test match. Like many England supporters, I feel I am a jinx to any chance they have of avoiding the ritual humiliation visiting sides invariably inflict upon them at Lord's and, now that I come to think of it, everywhere else in the world as well. The last time I went to Old Trafford two Englishmen scored centuries, but in countless days at Lord's, I have only ever seen one England batsman score a 50.

On the first day against India in 1986, Gooch scored a typically stylish 114. Unfortunately, I had tickets for the second day. And so my friend Nick and I turned up to watch D.R. Pringle plod to a grim, colourless 63. In all, 132 runs were scored that day, off 83 overs. It was punishingly boring. At tea we met some friends of Nick's for a drink, and tried to work out what sins we had committed to merit such barbaric treatment. Nick thought he may have filed a tax return late. I had recently been embroiled in a brief but doomed relationship, although I didn't think I had behaved that badly. But whatever we had done, Pringle was unquestionably the instrument of God's vengeance, sent to torture us into eating our sandwiches long before lunchtime. Even when he was out, our spirits did not lift. 'He'll be on to bowl soon,' said Nick, disconsolately nibbling the last banana.

The worst day was the Saturday of the Lord's Test in 1989, against Allan Border's all-powerful Australians. On Thursday England had scored 286 (R.C. Russell 64 not out, G.A. Gooch 60, D.I. Gower 57; M.G. Hughes 4–71).

Australia finished Friday on 276 for 6. Boon had made 84, Mark Taylor 62 and Steve Waugh was 35 not out. Australia were well placed but, as Bob Willis would say, there was all to play for. So on Saturday, I and three friends basked in unfeasible sunshine while Australia extended their first innings to 528. Steve Waugh finished on 152 not out, and could probably have scored another 300 had he received better support from the other end. As it was, Geoff Lawson scored a mere 74, Trevor Hohns 21 and Merv got a quick 30. The last 4 wickets added 263. England batted again and were swiftly 28 for 3. Not that I cared, for I had blotted out all feeling by that point with anaesthetic quantities of lager. At least Gatting hadn't shouldered arms, we giggled hysterically – although he did make amends for this shocking breach of tradition first thing Monday morning. As Bob Willis would say, it was all over bar the shouting.

Given all we know and all we have seen, you have to wonder why anyone bothers to go to Test matches. The standard theory is that it's to watch cricket, but any regular attendees can instantly point out the flaws in that argument. If you really wanted to watch cricket you would be at home in front of the television. The view is better, and it doesn't take twenty-five minutes to get to the lavatory. No, there has to be another reason. The problem is that, months after buying your tickets, you may struggle to remember what it was. One of the many conveniences of the credit-card revolution is that you now have to decide in February what you will want to do in July. Until a few years ago Lord's kept back a few unreserved seats for sale on the morning of the match. You would start queuing at 8.00 am, and be happily settled on your wet wooden bench by 10.30. But this provision was altogether too convenient and too popular for Lord's, which prefers to have your money safe and sound in its coffers, earning six months' interest. So the 8.00 am queues disappeared, and with them the layabouts and wastrels who prefer to act on a whim rather than plan their lives half a year ahead.

Still, for whatever reason we are going, we can't help but feel a frisson of anticipation on the morning of the match. All is ready for the great excursion. We have prepared the ground at work with strategic coughs and snuffles. We have bought our false moustaches to be worn in case our grinning features pop up on the *Nine o'Clock News*. We have wrapped our sandwiches in clingfilm, stored the chilled lagers in the cooler box, forgotten the suntan lotion, and now, at 10.35, we are walking along Prince Albert Road whistling the cricket TV theme tune.

This will be the day. England will turn this Test around, just as they have so often failed to do in the past. Inside the ground, everyone scurries around purposefully, for cricket is a serious business and it would not do to be seen to be taking it too lightly. In reality we are all a little light-headed, for there is no escaping the fact that this is a day off work, possibly unauthorised, in predominantly male company, with the prospect of gargles and banter galore, and the distant chance of a magnificent English recovery. If anything wonderful is going to happen, we want to be there to share the glory. If, as is more likely, abject failure is on the menu, we want to be first in with the rotten tomatoes.

I settle into my cosy plastic bum-contoured seat in the Compton Stand, and wait for Andy to turn up. The weather forecast is favourable – or at least it would be if you were a lizard, for temperatures are expected to edge into the eighties today, which for those of us on the top tier is roughly analogous to gas mark 5. It is 24 July 1994, the fourth day of the First Test against South Africa. A historic match, in fact, for England have not played South Africa in a quarter of a century. England's record in historic Test matches is not promising, and they are certainly making a hash of this one. South Africa scored 357 in their first innings, with a century from Wessels, crabbed and humourless as ever, and useful contributions from G. Kirsten, C.R. Matthews and J.N. Rhodes, amongst others. England managed just 180 in return. No one made more than Hick's 38 – a bad omen, for as Confucius say, whenever Hick is top scorer, defeat will surely follow. At the start of play on the fourth day, South Africa stand at 195 for 4, which means a lead of 372 – already substantially more than any team has ever scored in a fourth innings to win a Test match. The position isn't exactly hopeless, but it is fair to say that we are more likely to be besieged by armed terrorists today than see an England victory.

But England supporters are never deterred by poor results – which is just as well, for if they were, the game would curl up and die. In fact, considering the dire situation, the air of anticipation around the ground is remarkable. In my particular corner, however, it must compete with the air of ripe armpits wafting up from the row in front. By some mysterious law of crowd mathematics, fat sweaty men are shared equally around cricket grounds, so that everyone can have one. Ours is wearing an undersized T-shirt which, at only 10.50, already appears to be under intolerable pressure, both from the bulk it is struggling to contain and from his sweat glands, which must be pumping away like pistons. Fortunately, these new stands are well drained, although I wouldn't want to be sitting in front of him when the waters break around mid-afternoon. With some effort the fat bloke bends down to his cooler box and extracts a can of Heineken. The chilled *psscchht* makes everyone within a 20-yard radius feel thirsty. Only a trainspottery youth on my right seems unaffected. He is preparing his scoresheets for the day, and counting his felt pens. Andy can sit next to him.

The stand is filling up. To my left, a row behind, sits a dry stick, who has brought his small son along for what is presumably supposed to be a Treat. The son is looking restless. If this is a Treat, it's obviously not for him. 'Stop wriggling,' says Dry Stick, which is about as useful as telling him not to breathe. Meanwhile, immediately to my left, two middle-aged men in natty slacks have claimed their seats, and have whipped out what appears to be the first of an infinite supply of fish-paste sandwiches. This at least competes with the armpits, although the latter still have the upper hand. Between gummy bites, the Fish Pastes discuss team selection. 'Not sure about that Craig White,' says one. 'Don't think we should have New Zealanders playing for

England.' A minute later: 'What we need is a left-hander at the top of the order, like that Damian Bicknell, he's supposed to be quite good.' All we need now is for the Fat Bloke to take off his shirt.

I suddenly realise that I have left my own sandwiches at home. That will please Andy, as he is bringing the beer. But who needs food? Visions of that most blighted of foodstuffs, the TCCB cheeseburger, swim before my eyes. The umpires are walking out, followed by the fielders, followed by Peter Kirsten and Jonty Rhodes, and everyone is applauding politely. It is hard to get too passionate when you are 372 runs behind with 6 wickets yet to fall. Besides, it is already formidably warm. My ears are beginning to prickle. At least I have remembered the suntan lotion. I dig it out of my plastic bag and start smearing it across my few exposed areas of flesh. People look at me strangely. Suntan lotion? Hmm. Girls, homosexuals and Australians, maybe, but any true-born Englishman wielding a bottle of Factor 8 is somehow letting down the side. Far more manly to bare as much of yourself to the elements as possible. If you end the day with fourth-degree burns and inoperable skin cancer, then so much the better.

Kirsten is out, bowled Gough. Big cheers. 'Nothing like a good Yorkie in an England team,' says a Fish Paste on my left. 'Was that Rhodes or Gary Kirsten?' says the other. More *psscchhts* all around: we don't need much of an excuse to celebrate. Andy still hasn't arrived. I'm thirsty.

Rhodes is out, bowled Gough with what appears to be an inswinging yorker. Even huger cheers. 'Moved away in the air,' says a Fish Paste. 'At last!' shouts Dry Stick,

who is listening to *Test Match Special* on his headphones.
'Stop wriggling, can't you?' He obviously wants his son to
be inculcated in the ways of cricket, if only to give them
something to talk about, but he can't be bothered to do
it himself. He gives him the headphones. 'I think if you
listen to it on the radio, you might quite enjoy it,' he says,
shutting his eyes for a brief nap.

Fraser now picks up Richardson, caught behind. A
hundred and ninety-five for 4 has become 220 for 7.
The crowd rumbles with misplaced optimism. More cans
are opened. At this point Andy turns up, looking flustered.
Tube late, bad night, early morning meeting, etc. But I am
not bothered, as he has some sandwiches in his cooler box.
Meanwhile Fraser and Gough have come off, and DeFreitas
is bowling. No more wickets until lunchtime, then.

The play settles into a more familiar pattern: lots of
runs from Macmillan and Matthews, and not a sniff of
a wicket. Hick bowls tidily. The attention wanders. Only
the trainspottery youth seems at all animated, but then he
seems to have mislaid his green felt-tip pen. Andy, hero
of the hour, produces a chilled tinny from the depths of
his cooler box. The sweet evocative aroma of sausage rolls
wafts past our noses.

Eventually even Atherton is getting bored with this.
For him this is the calm before the storm: yesterday he
was caught with dirt in his pocket, and tomorrow the
recriminations will begin in earnest. For the moment,
though, he has a Test match to lose. Gough is brought
back and bowls Chris Matthews on the dot of lunch. 'Ah
yes,' says a Fish Paste. 'When Yorkshire are on top, England

are on top, that's what I always say,' ignoring the fact that England now need 456 to win. The other Fish Paste, in silent agreement, rolls up his slacks to reveal a fine pair of knobbly knees.

Wessels declares and the sandwich-munching begins in earnest, interspersed with a visit to the bar and a more pressing visit to the adjacent lavatory. Queues at both, of course, and as everyone is still relatively sober, we all stay silent. An Australian jumps the queue at the bar. Everyone stares at him disapprovingly, hoping that by doing so they can will him to conform to standard English behaviour. He doesn't even notice. I am back in my place by 1.30. Andy's chilled beers have to be held back for the dry hours between lunch and tea, but sadly all the banana sandwiches have gone.

England start comfortably enough, with Atherton, as ever, looking as though he could be out every ball, and Stewart looking so confident that you expect him to be out before Atherton. Dry Stick has perked up during lunchtime, possibly as a result of the bottle of wine he seems to have consumed since I last looked. 'Oh, well left!' he cries sarcastically, when Atherton plays and misses. This is a joke he quickly warms to. 'Oh, well left! Har har har!' His son has switched stations to Radio 1, but Dry Stick doesn't notice.

Meanwhile, Fat Bloke's T-shirt is losing its structural integrity as the rivers of sweat surge down his back. Can't be long now before he disposes of it altogether. Atherton is out, caught at second slip. Oh dear. Everyone sighs at the inevitability of it all. 'What a dreadful shot,' says Fish Paste

2. Later, on the highlights, it turns out to have been a very good ball, but we are not to know that now. Crawley is in and looks fearfully uncomfortable. 'Only a matter of time,' says Andy. Lots of cruel jokes about Manchester Grammar, Cambridge University, Lancashire Cricket Club and rectal passages, for the crowd is definitely warming up now. Fish Paste 2's knobbly knees are colouring nicely, having just passed orange scarlet on their way to angry puce. Crawley edges to slip – 29 for 2.

Some rows behind us, a T-shirted South African holding a can of Kronenbourg announces that he is holding a sweepstake. Guess England's score at close of play and whoever is closest wins the lot. 'No tax! No VAT!' No buyers at the moment, either, but then, try as he might, he can't quite keep the tone of triumph out of his voice. Hick has arrived and played two spanking shots for 4 off the back foot. 'Bound to get out now,' says Andy. Next ball Steve Randell gives him out lbw – a woeful decision, even from where we are sitting. (It looks even worse on the highlights.) Dry Stick is quite pissed by now, and yelling ironic abuse at each departing batsman. 'Oh well played, you moron. Pathetic. Fire the lot of you.' His son has stopped wriggling and started asking pertinent questions, but his father is having problems concentrating. 'National cricket team? What a joke. Wouldn't last ten minutes . . .' and so on.

We enter a phase of gripping defensive cricket, for Gooch has joined Stewart and both appear to be equipped to master the South African attack. As during any phase of gripping defensive cricket, the crowd gets twitchy. Fat

Bloke, who hasn't been heard to say anything all day, turns to his associate and mutters, 'It's a bit slow, innit?' Near the Tavern, a Mexican wave begins. Two circuits, and it is up and running. No one in the Pavilion acknowledges it, which amuses everyone briefly. But the suits in the corporate boxes are more enthusiastic than most, for they crave distraction from their business discussions and, more importantly, this tedious sporting event that until now has provided the only alternative entertainment. In our corner there is less support for the wave. Fat Bloke and his friend try to join in, but they are both in such a bad way that they only manage to stand up long after the wave has gone. Felt Pens is unaware of its existence. Andy and I both used to be rock journalists, and so are too cool to take part. The Fish Pastes are more enthusiastic, although when Fish Paste 2 stands up he has to bend his now empurpled knees for the first time in an hour, and yelps with pain. When the wave comes around again, Fish Paste 1 stands up by himself, but only half-heartedly. Thereafter his interest lapses. Dry Stick is too angry even to notice the Mexican wave. He cannot understand why Gooch and Stewart are playing so defensively. 'Hit the bloody ball!' he shouts over and over again. 'Disgrace to the nation . . . pathetic . . . bloody incompetents . . . Oh, well left, sir!' Most of us probably agree with everything he says – it's just that, ideally, we wouldn't choose him to say it on our behalf.

But then Stewart is caught behind and Craig White walks to the wicket. A cricket crowd can sense vulnerability in an instant. 'Four balls,' says Andy. 'An over,' say I. 'Three balls,' says Fish Paste 2. 'Five balls,' says a bloke behind. We're all wrong: he edges to slip first ball and trudges off again. As if on cue Fat Bloke finally gives in to temptation and removes his shirt. It is worse than we had feared. His back is covered by a thick carpet of black hairs which swoop and swirl like a tropical weather formation. Right in the centre, in the eye of the storm, sits a swollen red spot which could burst at any time. Andy and I move our belongings out of range. Soon Gooch is out lbw, falling over to leg in his familiar way. Eighty-two for 6. Can they reach 100?

You can pass through the whole gamut of emotions during a day like this. Enthusiasm. Excitement. Relief. Depression. Despair. Joy (when Hick scored those runs). Frustration. Fury. Violent hatred. As the afternoon wears on, the emotions become more muted as the warm lager blunts every response. Some, like Dry Stick, take the red-wine route, but by teatime you're a sad shadow of a man. There is, perhaps, only a small semantic gap between mid-afternoon snooze and loss of consciousness, but Dry Stick has breached that gap. His small son, whom I may have underestimated, is playing Tetris on his Gameboy and leaving his father to sleep it off. But even the lager drinkers are not feeling as well as they might. Every time we go to the loo, it seems further and further away, over increasingly impassable terrain. And we are now talking complete rubbish. My notes for this day become increasingly incoherent after teatime, when the bars reopen. There is no need for this to happen. Indeed, every year we go to a Test match determined that this year it won't happen. And then we hear the first *psscchht* of the day, and we know that a Coke won't do. The idiocy of it all is that we don't need to go to a Test match to do this. Why not just go straight to casualty, and cut out the middle-man?

The problem is our perennial, unquenchable optimism. It is always a shock to see England fail. We are sure that this time they will bury the opposition under a mound of runs. As we used to say in the 1980s, 'The show ain't over till the fat Botham sings.' We know they will probably lose, but we never quite give up hope.

This is why supporters at Test matches drink so much. Some commentators presume that the oil-tanker-floating quantities of beer, wine, Pimm's, champagne and, for all I know, methylated spirits sold at Test matches are consumed by a minority of brain-damaged thugs who only come to chant and cheer and wouldn't know a gully from a googly. But those are only the visible, violent drunks. Do not forget the silent majority of gloomy, mournful drunks. For every thug in a vest suggesting that Graeme Hick should be crucified on the superstructure of the Mound Stand, there are ten quietly pissed supporters like me who are too distressed by the day's events to do anything more than look down at our shoes and try manfully not to be sick on them. We're not the sort of people who would wish Hick to face so painful and undignified a death. A firing squad would be far more humane.

Gough is hit and retires hurt. DeFreitas, Salisbury and Fraser don't last long: 99 all out, and it's time to go home. Only Felt Pens, who did finally find the missing green one, is at all happy. For the rest of us, mirthless laughter is the only option. Three hundred and fifty-six runs isn't the largest winning margin in Test history. England aren't the worst Test side in the world. I'm not going to have a vicious hangover tomorrow morning. I'm not going to do this next year. Certainly not. Never again. Never again.

Andy just rang. How do I feel about the Friday this year? Yeah, OK . . .

CHAPTER FOURTEEN

Men in White Coats

Meditate on the lot of the professional umpire, and the words 'mug's' and 'game' spring instantly to mind. There you stand, day after day, your piles throbbing horribly – and for what? Angry glares from the bowler whenever you turn down his inane appeals. Silent contempt from the batsman, who knows you will get it wrong sooner or later. Audible contempt from the fielders, who claim catches whether or not the batsman hit the ball, and whether or not they caught it. Boos from the crowd when you go up to receive your commemorative medal. And general opprobrium from the rest of the country whenever you make a particularly rotten decision. Nowadays you can even see your particularly rotten decision replayed on a giant TV screen moments after you have made it – but by then it is too late, and Richie Benaud has already said, 'I'll let you make your own mind up about that one.' No wonder international umpires all have that wary, hunted look. It must take unfathomable reserves of mental strength – and in David Shepherd's case, about seven meals a day – just to keep going.

Still, as we all know, British umpires are the best in the world, unflappable men of sound temperament and unimpeachable integrity who never get it wrong, good Lord, no. It's pure bad luck that most recent home Test series have been characterised by a stream of particularly rotten umpiring decisions. For this reason the arrival of 'neutral' umpires (i.e., equally fallible souls who happen not to be British) has defused the tension rather wonderfully. When there are two British umpires giving lousy decisions, it looks like nationalistic bias. But when one of them happens to be a New Zealander, say, it's mere incompetence. At the other end the British umpire visibly gains strength from his 'neutral' chum's predicament. 'It's not my fault,' his broad grin seems to say. 'I wasn't there and I have an alibi to prove it.' Should the hurly-burly of the international circuit actually throw up an umpire who knows what he's doing, the British official seems to enjoy himself even more. Someone like the West Indian Steve 'Slow Death' Bucknor must give a fellow umpire great reassurance, especially as he is equipped with perhaps the longest index finger ever seen in these islands. When he sticks that in the air, you know you're out.

Ah, how we could do with officials of the integrity of

Shepherd and Bucknor in the Captain Scott Invitation XI. Every season – indeed, virtually every match – sees umpiring decisions so incredible that, on occasion, physical violence is only narrowly averted. Shepherd and Bucknor and H.D. 'Dickie' Bird would be the first to admit that they make mistakes. Most normal people would. But bad umpires never admit to mistakes. They merely make them, constantly. Bad umpires are like bad drivers: on no evidence whatsoever, they think they are the only people who know what they are doing. Look at the terrible driver jumping the lights or swerving to avoid stationary cars he hasn't noticed until the last moment. Whatever happens, whoever dies in a tangled heap of sizzling metal and plastic, it will always be someone else's fault. The bad umpire, cricket's equivalent, always thinks he is right and always turns out to be wrong.

A bad umpire preys on a batsman's mind. He sucks out confidence as a vampire consumes blood. Whatever your mental state as you walk out to bat, it only takes one glance up at a bad umpire to ask for middle-and-leg and you turn to jelly. 'Mustn't let it touch my leg! Mustn't let it touch my leg!' you scream silently to yourself. So you swipe wildly and are bowled. The bowler thinks he did it. Not so. It was the man in the white coat, his finger flexing in his pocket, ready for action, ready to ruin someone's day.

Several essential qualities make up the skilled umpire: eyesight, judgement, experience, calmness, intelligence, absence of malice and, not to be underestimated, the ability to count up to six. Bad umpires can only count up to five or seven; it is the seventh ball of the over that bowls you middle stump. Absence of malice is especially important, for the bad umpire does not care that you have driven fifty miles to play the game, that your dog died last week and that your wife has run off with your girlfriend. The bad umpire just thinks it would be very funny if he gave you out. Harry, whose search for the holy grail of the ultimate statistic will probably never end, recently looked through sixteen years of scorebooks to establish that three batsmen – Harry himself, Richard the Zen master and I – have accounted for over 75 per cent of all lbw decisions ever given against Captain Scott batsmen. By extraordinary coincidence, we are the only three batsmen in the team who make fond use of the forward defensive. Bad umpires loathe a well-executed forward defensive. (Some observers might consider it even more extraordinary that Harry would bother to look through sixteen years of scorebooks to find this out, but that is another matter.)

Bad umpiring naturally takes many forms. Some bad umpires specialise, say, in moral umpiring, or in sight-deficient umpiring. Others mix and match, according to mood. This is the Devil's own work, for, inevitably, bad umpires seem to have much more fun than their dully conscientious counterparts. Shorter life expectancy appears to be the only palpable disadvantage.

Moral Umpiring

As we have discussed, most of us lead our lives predicated on the notion that the laws of cricket are essentially, fundamentally correct. We may regard this as our strength; to the Moral Umpire, it is our weakness. The Moral Umpire has his own agenda. To the Moral Umpire, the idea of laws is pretentious in the extreme. What counts is not whether the batsman was out, but whether he deserved to be out. Pitched outside leg stump? Not important. Playing a bit boringly? Afraid so, and up goes the finger.

Terence, for example, has been umpiring for sixteen years, and refuses to accept that a ball that pitched outside leg stump cannot dismiss a batsman leg before wicket. 'It was going to hit the stumps,' he says reasonably, as the dismissed batsman rushes off to set fire to his belongings. He deserved to be out; the rules don't matter; the finger went up. 'It pitched outside leg stump,' I explain patiently for the 673rd time. 'Don't care abut that,' says Terence disdainfully. 'It was going to hit the stumps.'

There is no argument you can usefully employ against a Moral Umpire, for he knows he is right, in much the same way that you know he is wrong. Just make sure you get your own back when it's his turn to bat later on.

Get On With It

More of a subset of the Moral Umpire category than a category in itself, but nonetheless worthy of note. Get On With It is a non-batting bowler who thinks all batsmen are wimps because they don't try to hit every ball out of the ground. He probably comes in at 10 or 11, doesn't take a guard and aims a giant mow at every delivery, occasionally connecting with a few and, very occasionally, getting a quick 16 or 20. This makes him, in his tiny deranged mind, an all-rounder, but Get On With It still thinks like a bowler, and remains convinced that all bowlers get a bad deal. He regards the idea that batsmen should be given the benefit of the doubt as hifalutin nonsense. As an umpire, he gets rather more wickets than he manages as a bowler. Sample explanations include:

'He had his chance, didn't he?'

'It was such a good ball, it deserved a wicket.'

'Anyway, he was nearly out a couple of balls before.'

The Stickler

The direct opposite to the Moral Umpire, the Stickler knows the rules backwards and may even have Been on a Course. The Stickler enjoys giving people out as much as anyone, but is especially keen to give a batsman one short or no-ball a wicketkeeper who collects the ball a nanometre in front of the stumps. If you doubt the Stickler's word on anything at all, he will whip out a dog-eared MCC certificate of accreditation, which may even be real. But although the Stickler knows all the rules, and enjoys sitting in pubs with other Sticklers discussing abstruse cricketing conundrums, he is drastically lacking in judgement. His decisions are therefore just as crass as those of all the other bad umpires. Some forward-thinking Sticklers possess light meters, which they don't know how to use.

The Soft Touch

When in doubt, give in. If all the fielding team are shouting at the top of their voices, then it must be out, mustn't it? Soft Touch didn't hear the click himself, or spot a deflection, and the bowler did appeal that crucial five seconds after the wicketkeeper leaped into the air, and the batsman did look as though he may have clipped his pad, but they are shouting awfully loud, and not just, one assumes, because Soft Touch gave a terrible lbw in the last over. Up goes the finger, and two balls later, Soft Touch is quietly replaced.

Law of Averages

A variation on the above, represented in Scott's by Bob, our well-upholstered leg-spinner. Law of Averages likes to be liked, and after two or three lbw shouts he starts feeling that it would be unfair if he denied the bowling side indefinitely. Well, you can't turn them all down, can you? It's the law of averages, isn't it? Yes you can, Bob, and no it's not.

The Coach

A year or two ago, in a moment of disastrous vanity, we played the First XI of the North London school which Harry and I attended so many years ago. They destroyed us, of course, but not without the considerable assistance of their coach, who umpired throughout and used his position to instruct his batsmen how to play all our bowlers. Any shout for lbw was dismissively ignored, while at least one blatant caught-behind was shamelessly given not out. The Coach, short and unprepossessingly tracksuited, just kept on muttering, 'Wait for the bad ball – there'll be one along in a minute,' and pointing out the more incompetent holes in our field placings. When we came to bat, and prepared to provide an umpire of our own, he continued to insist on umpiring at both ends. Fortunately, a lugubrious Mancunian of our number, a TV producer of forthright views, reached the other end first. The Coach was apoplectic, but the Mancunian remained unmoved. 'I can count to six, you know,' he explained. When the Mancunian came into bat an hour later, the first ball hit his front pad many yards down the wicket. Extra cover appealed, and the Coach raised his finger with a huge grin on his face. The Mancunian, whose son was playing for the school, showed superhuman restraint in not describing the Coach as 'a cunt' until he was well out of earshot. Not that the Coach was bothered. He was the sort of bloke who signals leg byes when you've hit it off the middle of the bat just for the fun of it.

Teasing

A nasty habit, this. The bowler appeals, the Tease whips out his finger, appears to raise it to the heavens, and then, at the last moment, scratches his nose and mutters, 'Not out'. In the early 1980s my friend Brian made this his speciality. He never could resist an opportunity to make mischief, and umpiring offers as many opportunities as anyone could hope for. Once he played this trick on a striving young satirist as the fielding side loudly appealed for lbw. It was clearly not out, and Brian had no intention of giving it out, but before he had successfully completed the gag, the satirist marched up the field to berate (or possibly assault) Brian for the outrageous decision he thought he was about to make. The wicketkeeper then stumped him. Naturally Brian denied all blame, but no one laughed louder.

Home Advantage

Cricket teams like football teams, enjoy home advantage in small, intangible ways. They know how the wicket plays, they know where to place the field, they know whether or not to avoid the meat pasties in the local pub. But for some teams, mere local knowledge is never enough. What they need is a tame umpire, preferably a man of great cricketing knowledge and experience, with years of white-coat action behind him, sturdy of spirit and physique, and about as trustworthy as the Kray twins. So they call on Home Advantage, who is someone's grandfather and a stalwart of the cricket club these fifty years past. What a lovable old gent, everybody thinks, as he dons his tattered coat and ambles down to square leg. How easily visiting

teams are fooled. Run-outs: 'Sorry, didn't see that one.
There was someone in the way.' Lbws against home
batsmen: 'It's the slope, you see. There's no way that
I could give that one.' Lbws against visiting batsmen:
'That's out.' No-ball: screamed just as home batsman's
stumps fly out of the ground. Deafness: sudden attack as
home batsman is caught behind. Almost fatal coughing
fit: just as home batsman is stumped. What a character.
Loved by all. Never has to buy his own drinks in the pub.
I wonder why.

Blind

An obvious category, perhaps, but not a frivolous one. One
occasional player for Scotts is a wholly enthusiastic umpire.
When someone has completed his stint and no one else is
paying attention, he grabs the coat and almost sprints out
to the crease. He can count to six; he has no malice; he
chats happily to batsmen and fielders; he considers each
decision with due gravity; he gives virtually everybody out.
To use terms like 'white stick' and 'guide dog' would be
to disparage his enthusiasm – and yet moles would give
him a run for his money. Stevie Wonder would probably
have a clearer idea of whether the last ball pitched in line
with the stumps or not. He can't see a bloody thing. The
finger is raised, and another promising innings comes to
an untimely end.

CHAPTER FIFTEEN

August

In August, everything starts to fall apart. Regular players disappear on holiday, along with most of their potential replacements. To the few diehards who remain comes the realisation that opportunities to score that undefeated 88 or take those 6 quick wickets are rapidly being frittered away. Every game seems almost too valuable. It's my turn to bat. Hang on a minute, you batted for an hour and three-quarters last week. Everyone is tense. It's too hot. For months we have been complaining about the endless rain and cold; now it's too hot. Pitches are breaking up. Spinners are prospering. Our only decent spinner is playing golf. People are injuring themselves. Age is creeping up. No, it's roaring up behind us at 70mph. Spouses are tiring of the weekend grind and team-mates are tiring of each other. No drinks in the pub this week, got to get back. See you next Sunday. Sigh.

Sometimes I wonder if misery and gloom are endemic to cricket itself, or whether the game just attracts miserable, gloomy people. Glorious sunshine, hard wickets, amiable opposition – and yet everyone is moping around as though it's April. By now, of course, we have all spent three months together – long enough for mild irritation to grow into violent dislike and, if manipulated by the more Machiavellian members of the team, full-blooded hatred, with all its grisly consequences. In August it is not just Tim who looks as though he might hit someone, although, to be fair, he does maintain the 100 per cent dissatisfaction record of which he has become so proud.

The reasons for this decline are manifold. By August, Harry has probably been given out lbw on the front foot half a dozen times, each time by a Captain Scott umpire. As a bowler, he has had perhaps one back-foot lbw given him by an opposition umpire all season. Paranoia has set in. Against the quick bowlers, he is batting further and further out of his crease, and has become more jittery. He has probably lost form. So, as he always opens the batting, he is scoring fewer runs and taking longer over each of them. This in turn is infuriating the batsmen who come in after him. They seethe in the pavilion, none too subtly. Sooner or later one of them says, 'Right, I've had enough of this', grabs the umpire's coat, rushes out to the crease and immediately gives Harry out lbw on the front foot.

Then there are the new player–old player tensions, for by

now, new players have been playing for the team all season, and are beginning to settle in. But some old players, who perhaps don't play as much as they used to, feel that the new players are batting too high in the order or bowling too many overs. It doesn't help that when Harry is captain he tends to favour the newer cricketers, while I favour the old lags. They all look at each other, old players and new players, and wonder. Who are these people?

Selfishness. Hubris. Impatience. Truculence. To the poor harassed captain this can spell something very nasty indeed, for every decision he now makes is examined in microscopic detail. Everything you do as captain in August acquires layers of meaning identifiable only to the deeply paranoid, which essentially means anyone who hasn't bowled for a couple of weeks or who bats lower than number 5. Just take, as an example, the number of overs you give each bowler in an innings. Even at the best of times, bowling changes are a delicate matter. The number of overs a bowler bowls defines precisely his relative use to the team. So, for example, 1 over means that he is bowling purely for his entertainment qualities, probably in a match that is heading towards a tedious draw and needs a little livening up. If he concedes fewer than 12 in this over, everyone will be very disappointed. At least 3 wides are mandatory.

Two overs mean that he takes himself seriously as a bowler, but no one else does. If he is bowling pitifully and looks as though he may be taken off after his second, he may feign injury rather than suffer the gross humiliation of being withdrawn from the attack.

Three overs are mandatory for bad spin-bowlers, who may well take a wicket if you set a sensible field for them and they're lucky. Also for fast bowlers who have lost it and dodgy slow-medium swing-bowlers who always take a wicket or two in their first over and then get hit all over the place.

Four overs are the legal minimum for a 'real' bowler. Useful in a limited-overs match, when you can pretend that you will bring him back later for a second spell. Most bowlers always insist on one long spell because at village level second spells are as rare as umpires without an axe to grind. Four is also the maximum for ageing bowlers with troublesome knees.

Five is edging into respectability. Bowlers who are 'getting nowhere on this surface' often ask to be taken off after 5: the person whom they suggest as a replacement is the one whose average they would most like to see ruined. Five is also the absolute tops for Mr Try Anything Once, who may have got a couple of wickets and now wants to try his flippers and top-spinners, which are otherwise known as long hops and full tosses.

Six is about average for an opening bowler, especially one who takes himself very seriously. This means all opening bowlers, as they all take themselves very seriously indeed.

Seven overs mean he is either the captain's pet, or the captain, or we're desperate for bowlers. Quite terrible bowlers have sent down anything up to 15 overs in a single spell for Scott over the years.

But suppose you are playing in August, and there are

only four or five games left before the end of the season, and Harry gives Arvind 10 overs, and doesn't even take him off when he has taken 5 wickets. What's more, Harry put Arvind higher than you in the batting order, and he batted for 45 minutes and you only got 6 balls at the end. And (the final straw) Arvind tried to sell you some shares again during the tea interval. This would be tiresome enough in the spring. On August Bank Holiday, it is intolerable.

I speak from grim experience. I got my highest-ever score in August. To put this into some sort of context: for many years my highest score was 9. In 1980, our second season, I scored 9 in 50 minutes against Magdalen Flotsam, a ho-ho Oxford second team. In June 1982, I had again made 9 before Matthew wittily ran me out. My, how I laughed. In 1983, I improved on this – to 9 not out. This had moved beyond a joke, deep into the realms of tragedy. It wasn't until 1985, on a bastard of a pitch in Barnes, against a team called Villiers House, that I reached 12 not out. Bells pealed out spontaneously, and a ticker-tape parade through the streets of SW19 was seriously contemplated.

You can therefore appreciate what an extraordinary achievement it was when, two years later, I scored 35 against the same opponents. I opened the batting, got a couple of streaky 4s and, after the usual collapse, put on 67 for the 7th wicket with the striving young satirist. I had all but tripled my previous best score. I even timed a couple. Finally, with the game nearly won, I missed the inevitable straight one and wandered back to the huddle of Scott stalwarts nestling under a nearby tree. Total silence. A quiet 'Well batted' through gritted teeth from one of my oldest friends. Insincere smiles from some of the others. They were furious. By doing well, I had shown them up – and also prevented a handful of players from getting a bat at all. Most of the time I bat at 8 or 9, and have frequently gone a month or more without getting a bat myself. But that didn't matter. This was August. I shouldn't have expected anything else.

More recent Augusts have seen several guerrilla campaigns come to a head. One of the more entertaining involved Terence, this time in his capacity as wicketkeeper. Everybody wants to be wicketkeeper, because you can show off constantly and it's more fun than getting bored and cold in the outfield. I usually employ Terence, who, despite an almost total lack of aptitude for the job, loves doing it and is happy as a result to bat at number 11 – although for form's sake, he complains about this incessantly. Anyone who has ever captained a village cricket team knows the value of a player who is happy to bat at number 11. You nurture him, you indulge him, you sell him your sister at a knock-down price. Terence, of course, also gives me a lift to the game, which places his value beyond diamonds.

And, as if to prove that mediocrity is within the reach of all of us, he has become a perfectly serviceable wicketkeeper, of a sort. As an ex-goalkeeper, he has perfected the despairing dive to leg whenever one of our 'fast' bowlers momentarily loses control. He even takes a few catches. But the stumper's art has forever been beyond him. Blessed with reactions slightly slower than those of a dead dog, he collects the ball, moves his hands in the direction of the stumps, and triumphantly throws them down, only to find that it's time for tea and everyone has left the pitch. For many years he recorded only one successful stumping, when the batsman was so far out that he didn't make an effort to get back into the crease, but simply walked off towards the pavilion. Even then Terence nearly fumbled it.

Howard, our dashing number 3 batsman, wants Terence's job. He knows he is the better wicketkeeper, and proves it when Terence is absent, throwing himself around with crazed abandon, like Alan Knott on crack. But Howard is our dashing number 3 batsman, and would never contemplate a lower position even if it meant regular spells with the gloves. So he responds as only a village cricketer knows how: by subterfuge. He fields at slip, so when Terence misses a possible stumping, he groans theatrically and places his hands on his head. 'Woe is me!' his body language cries. 'That bloke would be halfway back to the pavilion if I had been behind the stumps!' Unfortunately for Howard, detailed observation of this mannerism has revealed that he does it whether or not the batsman stepped out of his crease at any stage. Even more unfortunately, Howard's taunting has prompted Terence to practise his stumping, which he would never have done before. Now, with a certain amount of encouragement from those team members who wish to rub Howard's nose in it, Terence has actually started taking the odd stumping in matches. Howard is now investigating more subtle ways of undermining Terence's position, such as arranging for him to be called away on business on the morning of the game.

But the most destabilising force of all in August is the

broken reed. As the summer wears on, a player who is having a bad season begins to wonder whether this may not just be a bad season. Perhaps such talent as he possesses has deserted him permanently. Perhaps he is not just woefully out of touch. Perhaps this is the beginning of the end. He wonders if everyone else on the team has come to the same conclusion. He wonders whether they now see him as a lame duck. A spent force. A broken reed.

In Captain Scott we know an awful lot about broken reeds. Players who once aspired to adequacy now find, a year or two later, that they are completely useless. Bowlers who used to take wickets now struggle to dismiss anyone past puberty. Batsmen who could be relied upon for a quick 15 now fail to stay in for more than an over. The reed is bemused. Why can't he do it any more? The eyes of his team-mates, meanwhile, drift inexorably to his midriff, where rests the evidence of a thousand business lunches. Cruelly planted behind a desk or the wheel of his company car for two-thirds of his waking hours, the reed has seen his youthful vitality trickle away, accompanied, in many cases, by his hair. His only consolation is that most of his team-mates are going the same way. Where once a proud team of chest-thumping supermen strode on to the pitch, there is now a paunchy, sad, dome-headed array of old crocks, quietly wheezing and spluttering as they limp out, heads bowed. On the sidelines sit their wives and girlfriends, looking worried. After all, the average age of the side is only thirty-four.

But while it's funny when this happens to someone else, it's a disaster if it happens to you. For years you have accepted your limitations as a sportsman; now, without warning, you are being asked to accept a whole lot more. This is a terrible moment for any male, for athletic prowess is inextricably tied up with machismo and, not to put too fine a point on it, willy length. Suffering a loss of this kind is like being athletically Bobbitted, without anaesthetic, and with all your friends watching. No wonder reeds always take it so badly. Usually they blame everyone else: fielders, wicketkeepers, umpires and particularly captains. 'Well, you know I'm no good against that kind of bowling,' a batting reed told me, even though, the season before, it had been exactly the sort of bowling he had enjoyed most. A bowling reed has taken to wondering aloud why 'it's not quite working today'. Once again his team-mates are far too well brought up to mention the mound of blubber now holding up his trousers, let alone the recent appearance of mighty love handles just above his generously proportioned buttocks.

You simply cannot ignore such questions of age and decay indefinitely, much as some people have tried. Old age is in the mind, they say, but in a cricket team it's also in the knees, in the eyes, and in the pub after the game. It's hard to accept because it seems so unfair. We are only in our early thirties. And yet the footballer Peter Reid was only a young buck of thirty-four when a tabloid newspaper described him as a 'time lord'.

Probably none of this would matter if we kept ourselves fit. But we are cricketers. We don't keep fit. If anything, we play cricket to avoid keeping fit. Fitness for cricketers is an optional extra – something that is nice to have but far less important than clean white trousers. We lead sedentary lives. I look at my friend Bob, the prosperously proportioned leg-spinner, who for many years supplied a backbone of pure incompetence that made Scott's lower-middle order a byword for fallibility throughout the Home Counties. When Bob graduated, a year or two after me, he was a bright, wiry, energetic character, bursting with ambition. These days he is in danger of an entirely different sort of bursting. Years of Indian meals, cheap red wine and 3.00 pm lie-ins have altered his body chemistry at the molecular level. After an averagely excessive lunch his face acquires a purple tinge that clashes horribly with his bloodshot eyes. In the face of constant media pressure to 'live a healthier lifestyle', he is an example to us all.

But such a devil-may-care attitude to physical fitness can only rebound on you. Until I was thirty, I thought only real sportsmen had injuries. Tim was forever twisting and pulling things, but we all thought he was just showing off. Now none of us can run up a flight of stairs without pulling hamstrings or tearing ligaments. And injuries don't just clear up as they used to. A dozen years ago I played a truly pitiful square cut which missed the ball completely and, in the process, momentarily wrenched my shoulder from its joint. It was breathtakingly painful for a split-second, but it popped back straight away and I carried on batting. It was more of a shock than anything else. I experienced no more pain, although it twinged a bit the following day.

Then, last August, I did exactly the same thing. Inept ill-timed shot, the shoulder momentarily springs out, springs back, absolute agony for a moment, shock, carry on batting,

out feebly three balls later. Only this time the pain did not
go away. This time my shoulder was aching constantly for
five weeks. I moaned about it incessantly. Why wouldn't it
get better? 'Because you're a sad old bastard,' said Harry,
and he was right.

Age is of course no barrier to a long and fruitful
cricketing career. We used to play against a team run by
a distinguished actor of advanced years who, despite the
presence in the side of many a fiery young thespian, always
opened the bowling himself. No one argued. It was his
team. Opening batsmen approved of the arrangement too.
You had to admire his bravado, not to mention his absolute
indifference to being hit all over the place week after week.
He loved playing, and was damned if he was going to allow
mere decrepitude to stop him turning out every Sunday. In
the end he refused to play us after Harry and Francis, the
merchant banker, came to blows on the pitch, but as long as
the fixture survived, we recognised him as a kindred spirit.

Is this a consolation? The well-tended body can carry on
playing cricket until it drops, but your peak is over before
you know it. In August, holiday-related gaps in the team
make it imperative that Harry finds some new players.
Some of them are as elderly as the rest of us, one or two
even more so. Some are rather younger. The broken reeds
slouch gloomily in the pavilion, watching sharp young
players score unbeaten centuries and win the match by
8 wickets. For these and other reeds, August has delivered
its seasonal double whammy: the imminent end of another
unsatisfactory season, and the slightly less imminent end of
another unsatisfactory life. After you with the razor blade.

CHAPTER SIXTEEN

Foreign Fields

I have played against Lazio, and lost. Admittedly it was only Lazio Cricket Club – the football team were otherwise engaged that day, beating Parma 5–2. It was October 1992, and we were in Rome on the annual Captain Scott Invitation XI foreign tour. The spread of cricket across the civilised world – promoted largely by a diaspora of cricket-crazed Sri Lankans, it seems – has made it increasingly practicable for shambolic sides of British no-hopers to fly almost anywhere and get beaten by foreigners. So far we have visited France (three times), Spain, Italy and, in early 1994, Hong Kong and India, for a wallet-bashing fortnight in the mystic East. Everywhere we go, we are ritually crushed by teams of super-fit athletes who assume that because we have flown all that way we must be good at cricket. How little they understand the British psyche. We have flown all that way because we are able to fly all that way. Talent has nothing to do with it.

So it was that on Saturday 3 October 1992, we found ourselves in the middle of Rome's famous Capanelle Racecourse, playing the Capanelle Cricket Club on a concrete and matting wicket. Every fifteen minutes or so, another dozen horses would gallop behind the bowler's arm, briefly delaying play. Quite what the small crowd of Italian horse-fanciers thought of these foreign fools in immaculate whites and matching yellow-and-blue caps will never be known. No doubt they were far more concerned with the likely prospects of Bee's Knees (or its Italian equivalent) in the 2.30. We knew we were an incongruous sight. Lacrosse players in the middle of Glorious Goodwood could not have felt more out of place.

Come to Rome in October, they said. That's when the weather is at its finest, they said. Warm and balmy, with a pleasant breeze; temperatures no higher than the mid-seventies. Not the remotest chance of rain, let alone unseasonal tropical storms that have taken the wrong turning at Gibraltar. So it was with the inevitability of a dropped slip catch that massive stormclouds foregathered above us halfway through the afternoon. Since lunchtime our regular côterie of amateur meteorologists had been studying faraway cloud formations and talking ominously of cumulonimbus thunderheads. We were all agreed: it was only a matter of time. We batted first, and accumulated runs with typical drabness. The sky gradually darkened,

and as the wickets fell, the clouds began to race across
the sky as though late for an appointment. I myself fell
first ball, fooled by a straight one. I had been on holiday
on the east coast of Italy, sharing a house with a group of
friends that included Terence and Stephen. We had driven
hundreds of miles, and added hundreds of pounds to the
cost of our holiday, just to play these two games. Terence
lasted one ball; Stephen made it to three. By now the
whole city was shrouded in a preternatural murk. Old
cricketing heads, especially those who had survived the
Finchingfield hailstorm of 1985, looked to the sky and
awaited the deluge.

We didn't have long to wait. Barely had Stephen,
Terence and I put the finishing touches to our ducks
than the monsoon began. Everyone huddled under a tiny
straw sunbreak, or the 'pavilion', as we had fondly come
to know it. We might as usefully have sheltered under
a handkerchief. After twenty minutes we were drenched
in that thorough, all-pervading way that makes it hard
to imagine that you can ever be dry again. Then, as
suddenly as it had started, the rain stopped. We wandered
out tentatively. I volunteered to field in the shallow end.
But the storm was only pausing for breath. A minute later
it bucketed down again, and we legged it to the changing
room. That morning, we later heard, the local fire brigade
had been placed on flood alert.

An hour or two later, we settled down for a lengthy
meal with our thoroughly hospitable opposition. Outside
it was still belting down. Tomorrow's game against Lazio
was bound to be cancelled. Eat, drink and be merry, for

tomorrow we shall do a little cursory sightseeing. Buckets
of red wine were therefore ordered and consumed, and
that strange madness that afflicts the British when they
are abroad in large groups took hold of us. On and on
the evening went, with several random changes of location.
Tim had heard a rumour that Gazza drank in a particular
bar on the other side of the city; we set off to find it.
All tours involve at least one daft excursion of this sort
that ends in failure and recrimination, and this was it. We
ended up somewhere, talking about something, and I got
to bed at about 4.00 am.

The following morning wasn't such fun. My own hangover was a blaster, bad enough for me to glean no
amusement at all from the discovery that several other
people felt even worse. More ominously, few of us could
fail to observe the presence of a huge yellow orb in the
sky, drying up the puddles and mocking our presumptions
of the previous night. The game was on. It would start on
time. Eleven o'clock.

As we arrived at the ground, it would be an exaggeration
to say that we were enthusiastic. In some cases we weren't
even conscious. Miserable Bill Matthews, who even at the
height of his glooms retains some of the skin pigmentation
he inherited from his Asian forefathers, was blanched
white. Everyone had forfeited at least one of their five
senses. Quick singles seemed an unlikely prospect.

In fact, to begin with, things didn't go too badly. Lazio
put us in to bat on a drying matting wicket, and after
the usual fall of early wickets our tempo began to pick
up. Ian Wall, who had tested his sturdy constitution to

its very limits, became the first batsman in Captain Scott history to throw up at the wicket while making 78 not out. On balance, 167 for 7 after 30 overs appeared a reasonable total. (Terence, Stephen and I, needless to say, didn't face a ball.)

But fielding was another matter. Standing up for an over at a time was a challenge. Sprinting insouciantly over from cover point to intercept a firmly struck off-drive wasn't even on the table. And Italians bat as they do everything else: like lunatics. If it's up there, they hit it. Actually, wherever it is, they hit it. Unlike most cricketing outposts, the Italian club system requires that at least seven home-born cricketers play in every game, even friendlies. Foreign players are not allowed to bowl together or, unless there is no alternative, bat together. As a result the Italians don't just make up the numbers, they really can play. They passed our total with 7.5 overs to spare.

That evening we really relaxed, which made for an interesting flight home the following day. Hundreds of pounds for no runs, two hangovers and a shocking cold that hung around for weeks. Apparently, this is what touring is all about.

Abroad. As a three-year-old of my acquaintance recently assured me, it's a big place. The risk in going there, sadly, is that the local populace may neither know nor care why anyone should wish to shine one side of a cricket ball and not the other. Much as we may love the Germans and esteem the doughty inhabitants of Belgium, we have to admit that their understanding of reverse swing is at best limited. Christ, you can feel lonely in those places. All of us, at one point or another, have sat in featureless hotel rooms, very possibly in Rotterdam, desperate to know the Test score but unable to pick up anything on the television other than MTV. We ring Reception. 'Any chance of BBC2?' Sadly not. 'Er, Radio 3 medium wave?' Sadly not.

Perhaps the greatest examination of one's mettle, though, is the family holiday. In your twenties you can generally avoid this by the ingenious ruse of not getting married. With rare foresight I have managed to extend this run of luck well into my thirties, but many friends of mine enjoy the full pleasures of a domestic existence, of which the family holiday is an annual highlight. Suddenly all the horrors of childhood return, with the additional horror that you are now paying for it all. Two prime weeks of the cricket season are thus needlessly sacrificed at the altar of marital harmony – and all because school terms start in the same week as the NatWest final. Why people won't take their annual fortnight's break during sunny November defeats me.

So, to the airport, where you notice there could be the makings of a good matting wicket in between the runways. Through Customs and Passport Control, where you notice that the man checking the passports looks uncannily like 'Flat' Jack Simmons. Should you say 'Hello, Jack,' on the off-chance that it is indeed the world-famous Lancashire off-spinner? The risk is that so many people have done this in the past that he may refuse to let you through. You hold your tongue. In the departure lounge, you make straight for the bookshop, where you purchase a variety of improving tomes. A recently retired player's autobiography. An expensive reprint of a 1930s' book of whimsical cricketing reminiscences. P.G. Wodehouse's *Psmith in the City* (1910). You open this latter. Young Mike Jackson is toiling away in his menial job at the New Asiatic Bank when his county captain brother Joe rings up.

'Look here, Mike, are you busy at the bank just now?'

'Not at the moment. There's never anything much going on before eleven.'

'I mean, are you busy today? Could you possibly manage to get off and play for us against Middlesex?'

You recoil, horrified. This is pure cricket porn – not the sort of thing you want to be reading at the start of an enforced fortnight's break at the height of the season. You return to the *Telegraph* sports pages with relief.

At the airport at the other end, the customs man looks disturbingly like Farokh Engineer, and the taxi driver is the absolute spit of K.D. Walters. The hotel is very nearly finished, although the indoor nets your travel agent promised turn out not to exist. You turn to the cricketer's autobiography. It is ghost-written by a man from the *Daily Star*, and details our hero's endless battles against blinkered officialdom, fickle selectors, insensitive journalists (presumably not including the man from the *Daily Star*), selfish team-mates, hostile crowds, sledging fast bowlers with huge moustaches, biased umpires, incompetent agents, predatory bimbos and the drug squads of three continents, while claiming on his behalf total innocence

on all counts and assuring his loyal readership that he
has never even met the air hostess in question. He owes
it all to his loyal wife, Sharon, or at least he would do
if she ever filed for divorce. He and his family now live
peacefully in the country, breeding horses and waiting for
the panto season. And the catarrh has cleared up very
nicely, thank you.

Isn't the weather wonderful today? Hey, let's play a game
of something on the beach. Frisbee, perhaps, or boules?
Or beach cricket, as you just happen to have a tennis ball
and a tennis racket back at the hotel? Oh come on, just a
quick game.

You notice that the sand takes spin from the first ball.
Your wife can't score runs on the off side. Your six-year-
old daughter is curiously vulnerable to the well-directed
bouncer. Bowled first ball, you call a no-ball because there
are more than two seagulls behind square on the leg side.
You bat on for the rest of the day.

After two games like this, in which you score 154 and 128
not out, your family refuse ever to play with you again. You
go in search of like-minded souls whose families have also
rejected them in this heartless fashion. Especially if these
like-minded souls have access to a proper kiddies' cricket
set, complete with plastic stumps.

No luck, so you pick up the 1930s' reprint. 'What strange
charm there is in the hollow echoes of a cricket pavilion!'
you read. No, perhaps later.

After two weeks of hell, you and your bronzed brood
pack up and return, although not before you see someone
in the street who looks astonishingly like Alvin Kallicharran.

Back in Britain, they have enjoyed the best weather of the summer. You tell everyone you had a great time. Not even your children believe you.

The most disastrous Captain Scott excursion of all combined the dynamics of a cricket tour (male bonding, alcohol, cheap hotels, desultory sightseeing) with the duration and cost of a real holiday (two weeks, and don't ask). The plan was simple: a week in Hong Kong, a week in Delhi, two games in each. Francis, our high-flying merchant banker, was then working in Hong Kong, and so arranged that leg of the operation. Arvind fixed up everything in Delhi. It seemed a wonderfully crazy idea. Damn the expense: we'll never have an opportunity to do anything like this again. A dozen players, two wives and two girlfriends signed up. We had our injections, queued up at India House for our visas, bought the guidebooks. We flew out of Heathrow full of hope and excitement, not to mention duty-free.

By the time we returned, thirteen days later, virtually no one was talking to anyone else. Small groupings of people who now loathed each other tactfully avoided saying goodbye while they grabbed their luggage and fled to waiting cabs. At Delhi Airport earlier, at least one punch had been thrown. Arguments over money – and we're talking pathetically small amounts of money here – had raged, and, as I write, have still not been entirely resolved: one debt for £42 remains unpaid. I myself could barely bring myself to spit the names of at least five of the returning personnel, while my girlfriend, who had also come on the trip, wanted to murder at least eight. Six days later, she gave me the elbow. I developed amoebic dysentery. Credit-card companies wrote pointed letters. It was quite a trip.

Considering the whole nasty business with the benefit of a year's hindsight, I have to admit that I was as much at fault as anyone. The main argument arose over the choice of hotel in Delhi. Arvind, asked to save money, had booked us into the sort of accommodation normally shunned by all but the most desperate cockroaches, and only those who had been offered a special deal. One team member observed that the cleanest place in his room was the ring under his water jug. At least two players could not find it within themselves to undress to get into their beds, so grey and ripe were the sheets.

And so, in a declaration of UDI, five of us upped and checked into the Hyatt Regency. There we enjoyed blandly international levels of luxury, which were just the ticket after the Hotel Armpit. Those who stayed behind were unimpressed. In fact, they were livid. Relations between the two parties declined. Only Cie, our off-spinning legend, behaved with any dignity over the next few days, his unfailingly good nature rendering him immune to the madness. But the rest of us . . . well, you don't want to know the details. Let us just say that words were spoken, as well as yelled, hurled and spat, and the social fall-out poisoned much of the following season.

Could this have been foreseen? Does Mike Gatting eat cheese and pickle sandwiches? Throw together a motley selection of yobs, thugs and know-alls, add a handful of volatile girlfriends, mix in one or two previously unarticulated antipathies, season with culture shock, and give the mixture a good stir. Then charge a fortune for the whole thing. The cricket tour is a rich dish indeed. If consumed without care, it can ruin your digestion for life.

Ah, the irony. As I am writing this, I am also trying to arrange our next tour, somewhere even more exotic, somewhere even sillier, where every potential opposition will mash us to a pulp. We must be out of our minds.

But for a writer, no experience is ever wasted. It is with this in mind that I have devised the Cricket Tour Game, which can be played by anyone venturing abroad for spurious cricketing reasons. Score points as instructed, and add up your total. Depending on your point of view, anyone scoring over 200 has done either very well or very badly indeed.

Part 1: At the Airport

You have met at the airport with all your cricketing chums. Score 1 point for any player not there on time. Score 3 points for any player subsequently found hiding in the bar. Score 5 points for every passport that has to be retrieved from a piece of luggage which has already been checked in. Score 10 points for every piece of cricket equipment that goes missing in the process.

Part 2: On the Aeroplane

Long haul, short haul, it doesn't matter. As far as the cricket tourists are concerned, it's time for a drink. Score 4 points for every drink consumed before pubs in England would normally open. Score 5 points for any player who asks for a chaser. Score 1 point for any player who snores loudly during the film. Score 1 point for any player who tries to chat up the stewardess. Score 1 point for each filled barf bag.

Part 3: At Your Destination

Score 2 points for each lost passport, piece of luggage, item of clothing left on plane, etc. Score 5 points for each argument with a passport official ('Can't you read? I am a British subject.'). Score 5 points each time you pass the same landmark in the taxi on the way to the hotel. Score 10 points for each argument with cab driver. Score 3 points if you have hot water in your room. Score 3 points if you have a window.

Part 4: At the Match

Score 5 points for each humorous 'local rule' dreamed up by the opposition to hamper your efforts. Score 2 points for every terrible lbw decision. If in the Indian subcontinent, score 10 points for every serious stomach ailment contracted from lunch. Score 1 point for every foreign passerby who stops to look at you as though you are mad. Score 1 point for every 36-shot film of useless 'action photos' you take. Score 5 points for any player who forgets his cap and contracts mild sunstroke.

Part 5: Sightseeing

Score 10 points for every player who claims to be fluent in the local language. Score 200 points for every player who really is fluent in the local language. Score 1 point for each unnecessary item you buy, plus an extra point if you have been gratuitously ripped off for it. Score 15 points for each unnecessary item you later manage to palm off on an unsuspecting friend or relative.

Part 6: Late-Night Entertainment

Score 25 points for any player (without wife or girlfriend present) who says that he fancies an early night tonight, if that's all right by everyone, and he'll see them all at breakfast. Score 5 points for any player who manages to get through the evening without buying a drink. (Score an extra 50 if that player is you, but only if no one notices.) Score 5 points for anyone who pompously pronounces on the intrinsic superiority of the local beer. Score 2 points for any player who decides to try a local liqueur, 2 more if he pretends to like it, 20 points if he actually likes it. Score 1 point for any player telling any other player at three in the morning, 'You know, Cliff, you're a fucking good bloke, you really are.'

Part 7: Blow-Up

Score 1 point for every punch thrown. Score 1 point for every swear word. Score 50 points if you manage to keep out of it completely.

Part 8: The Journey Home

Score 5 points per argument, plus an extra 5 if it is with the cab driver again and an extra 10 if the police have to be called. Score 1 point for every player drunk before he gets on the plane. Score 5 points for every player 'accidentally' tripped up in the aisle on his way to the loo. Score 2 points for every player who said he definitely ordered the vegetarian meal, even though you know he didn't. Score 1 point for everyone who says we saw this film on the trip out. Score 1 point for each lost passport, piece of luggage, etc. at the airport. Score 50 points if you speak to any of them ever again.

CHAPTER SEVENTEEN

In the Bleak Midwinter

'Smart casual': the mode of dress designed expressly for social occasions that are neither smart nor casual. An annual cricket dinner, for instance. Even though, a couple of months after the end of the season, the summer's emotional wounds have not entirely healed, at least enough of a scab has formed to allow for an evening's shared jollity in a private room of an overpriced restaurant whose food you won't notice unless it is spectacularly inedible. Another magnificent season has come to an end. I took two catches, dropped loads more, captained the team heroically to six victories, happened to be captain while the team suffered eight defeats, and scored a highly creditable 34 runs at 4.50 (top score 10 not out). Everyone is here. Tim is in one of those ebulliently good moods that cannot last, if only because they have never lasted yet. Our imposing leg-spinner Bob is telling everyone he plans to play far more next season, which fools nobody. (He cannot resist the call of the golf course for long.) As the evening begins, with a quick drink in a nearby pub, we are all consciously on our best behaviour. Let's have a good time. Let's not get too rowdy or offensive this year. After tonight, most of us won't clap eyes on each other for six months. Save the grudges for the first game of the next season, and pray that the seating plan works in your favour.

Such optimism. Cricket-club dinners are all different and all the same, with a strong emphasis on drunken cheering and ritual humiliation. And yet they serve an important purpose, for our tidy minds demand a neat, identifiable end to the season, something the season itself can never actually provide. The last game is always a monumental anti-climax. It is your last chance to excel, although in the event, it usually proves to be your last chance to fail as well. Sometimes you do not even get that. We used to end the season at a particularly beautiful village in Oxfordshire, whose vicious, relentless team always beat us resoundingly. As far as I am aware, the only time we inflicted any sort of defeat upon them was when I won a bottle of British sherry in their pub raffle in the early 1980s. In those days we played them towards the beginning of the season; by 1990 we had been relegated to the last weekend in September, long after the swallows and Ray Illingworth had flown south for the winter. Arriving there on an unseasonally clement day, we found an odd and disconcerting lack of opposition. Not only was there no one in the pub (although that's hardly surprising, as around two-thirds of all village teams have fallen out with the landlord of their local pub, and drink somewhere else fifteen miles away), but the pitch wasn't marked out, stumps were nowhere to be seen and, crucially, there were no gigantic piles of sandwiches wrapped in tinfoil in the pavilion. Phone calls were made. 'Oh no, old son,' explained the fixtures secretary, improvising skilfully, 'one of your chaps rang up two weeks ago and cancelled the game.' A motion from a perennially angry fast bowler that we burn down the fixture secretary's house was narrowly defeated, so we ended up playing one of those sad games of softball that so often beset stranded cricket teams in these circumstances – the sort of game in which only two people know the rules and argue furiously over every alleged infringement.

Driving home later, we realised we had been foolish to be so disappointed. Cricket seasons always end in disarray, and to get a game of softball out of the day was more than we could ever have bargained for. Usually you just waste a day indoors, staring furiously out of the window, waiting for the rain to stop. Then, the day after the last fixture, a glorious Indian summer begins. Everyone wears shorts and sunglasses again; the swallows turn round and fly back; the weathermen say there's more to come. And still you stay indoors, staring furiously out of the window, waiting for the rain to start again.

The end of the season also produces Harry's comprehensive statistical digest, which proves once again that the best players are better than the ones who aren't any good. With luck there will be two or three people below me in the batting averages, although since Harry's previous girlfriend stopped playing for the team I have been denied the cushion she regularly provided between me and last place. Stephen, who delights in the role of official worst player – either you delight in it, or you connect the hosepipe to the exhaust – now seems to have taken up permanent residency in last place, which I can't help feeling is terribly kind of him. Without his selflessness my own record of avoiding last place every year for sixteen years would surely be under threat.

More entertaining are the results of the Captain Scott Fantasy League, which we ran for the first time in 1994 and which seems certain to keep us amused for the rest of our lives. Last year there were twenty-four teams in the league, all made up of regular and semi-regular Captain Scott personnel. Our token Aussie Steve Mills finally won by dint of being the only person to pick Arvind. You gain Fantasy points whenever your chosen players score a certain number of runs, take wickets or take catches, which made for some interesting scenes later in the season, as the league reached its gripping climax. If someone took a catch, he was immediately mobbed by all the players who had chosen him for their teams, and sulkily ignored by all those who hadn't. And when a steepling aerial catch looked likely, fielders shoulder-charged each other out of the way in order to be the one to catch it. There's nothing like enthusiasm, especially when there's £100 at stake.

Both the statistical digest and the Fantasy League results are circulated at the dinner, and provide useful fuel for the real business of the evening, the gladiatorial points-scoring that masquerades as conviviality on all such occasions. As at the pre-season jolly, it only takes a few bottles of wine for the atmosphere to decline into the usual cut-and-thrust of rancour and bile. Some players, not surprisingly, don't like it at all. A couple of years ago the floppy-haired heart-throb, then awaiting his giant leap to megastardom, received unconscionable stick for a series of tabloid newspaper reports which alleged that he had rejected the advances of a certain carnally inclined American pop goddess. So enraged was he by this treatment that he made his excuses and left. 'Can't stand the heat,' we all chortled, dead jealous that none of us had been propositioned by the rumpily minded songstress in question.

At the end of the dinner, when everyone's critical faculties are at their most diluted, I hand out my annual awards for excellence. The Bill 'Chariots of Fire' Hoath Memorial Rolling Pin for the Most Henpecked Player. Fattest Player of the Year (given to the player who would be most offended at receiving the award). The Tom Cairns Award for Worst Bowler. Baldest Player of the Year (see Fattest Player). And so on. Institutionalised cruelty enjoys a central role in all primitive cultures, and there aren't many cultures more primitive than a cricket team.

And so, as we subside happily into our minicabs, the cricket season is officially closed. Time to fumigate the sports bag and humanely destroy any stray socks that linger within. Time to take stock. Time, at last, to think of something else. Rather too much time, in fact, to think of something else.

Summer is over in a moment; winter lasts forever. The worst winter days will be those crisp cloudless ones when the sun shines, the dew glistens and the cricket fan, not unnaturally, thinks of cricket. Why can't we play on days like this? Given that we venture out in the most uncompromising April squalls, you have to wonder why cricket is not played all year round. Footballers don't regard the calendar as any sort of encumbrance, while lunatics covered in whale grease regularly go swimming in the Serpentine on Christmas Day. Playing cricket on Christmas Day wouldn't be a fraction as mad as that, although I am not altogether convinced by the whale grease. In April and September, at the fag-ends of summer, we tolerate vicious extremities of cold. We rub our hands together and run on the spot in doomed attempts to keep warm. Yet we would not consider not playing. Cold hands drop hard balls, but that's just something you have to put up with. We love to play when the summer sun shines and the annual hosepipe bans are in full force, but we square this with the need to play when the weather is more brutal – which in a poor summer might be 80 per cent of the time.

So why not extend the jollity all the way to December and January, when we really would have something to complain about? Christmas fixtures at The Oval would presumably present few problems for the groundstaff. There would be no chance of the pitch breaking up. On the contrary, you'd need a pneumatic drill to make any impression. Fielders could glide across the outfield, sometimes literally, if they were wearing skates. And I can't believe that the dozen rain-or-shine lunatics who watch every County Championship match would notice that it was thirty or so degrees colder.

It will never happen. The psychology of sporting misery is too powerful. This is why the British are so good at inventing sports, or adapting sports to make them worse, because we understand so well the psychology of sporting misery. The football season has to go on all year because the nightmare of following a useless football team must be never-ending. Without the relentless momentum of crapness, the illusion that football has any purpose at all would swiftly crumble.

Cricket is different. It is the 'summer game'. If the summer weather turns out to be slightly less clement than a bad night on Cape Horn, that's just bad luck. But if the winter turns out to be twice as warm and sunny as the summer, that's also bad luck. It's no coincidence that it always rains solidly for the last two weeks of the season, or that a balmy Indian summer always kicks in the following day. Such ironies are small beer to anyone who has ever been caught out on the boundary by an eight-year-old. We all know that those crisp cloudless December days would be ideal for cricket – not especially warm, admittedly, but bright and windless enough to keep you alert. It's because they would be ideal that we can never play them. There must always be too much football; there must never be enough cricket.

In the bleak midwinter, there is only one way to satisfy the craving, and that's the most desperate method of all: following England's overseas tour on BBC Radio and satellite TV.

These are the dark days for the English cricket fan. True, the England team always set out with the hopes of a nation behind them, hopes that are dashed only when they take the field for the first match. But the days would be dark even if they were scoring 500 an innings and bowling out the opposition in 20 minutes. It has nothing to do with cricket. It's just that we spend so much time awake at night listening to it on the radio or watching it on TV that we pass most of the daylight hours fast asleep.

This problem of nocturnal sport can be severely injurious to the health, and no doubt a hard-hitting BBC2 documentary on the subject is being prepared at this very moment. Of course, it does depend on where England are going. Of all the locations on offer, India and Pakistan are perhaps the most civilised, for play starts there halfway through the night, allowing you to set the alarm for a reasonable hour – say 4.30 am – and enjoy the familiar spectacle of Hick being out for 0 over an early bowl of high-energy Wheatie Puffs. Australian tours are less forgiving. In typical awkward beer-swilling antipodean style, Australia has insisted on positioning itself in the world's most inconvenient time zone, which means start of play at bedtime and stumps at dawn. It is at times like this that cricket fans give grateful thanks for Perth, which is two hours nearer to civilisation. And thank heavens for day–night matches, which take us most of the way to lunchtime. But even Australia is not as potentially harmful to one's physical wellbeing as the West Indies, where the sporting day starts temptingly at eight o'clock in the evening. True, this allows us to enjoy the sight of English batsmen having their noses smeared all over Sabina Park for several precious hours every night. But what if the play is especially enthralling? Oh, I'll just watch another half an hour. Oh, perhaps another ten minutes. Just up to the tea interval, then ... Before you know it, the morning sun is gleaming through the curtains and it's Wheatie Puffs time again. Good for your bowels, all that fibre, but it adds up to weeks of nearly constant jet-lag.

A few years ago, before Sky Sports, our lifeline to civilisation was BBC Radio. This was altogether a more furtive cricketing experience, often proscribed by parents who felt there was something faintly grubby about staying up all night listening to Christopher Martin-Jenkins. While other teenagers were enjoying normal, healthy teenage activities, like non-stop masturbation, we cricket fanatics were lying in our beds with our pitiful little transistors and our earpieces, groaning with despair every time an England wicket fell. Only much later did I realise that a groan of despair sounds like any other sort of groan, which explains some of the odd looks I used to get from my parents and their surprise that I didn't possess wrists like high-tensile steel.

Nonetheless, my addiction to night-time *Test Match Special* continued long into adulthood. I discovered that late at night was an excellent time to do some desultory work, or 'work' as it should perhaps be more accurately described, as I never really did any. I would get as far as switching on the computer, but sixty-three games of Solitaire later, I usually switched it off again. The important thing was to avoid damaging your radio in any way at all. Needless to say, this is precisely what I did in a fit of anger when England were being mashed on the 1990–1 Ashes tour. One moment I was listening to Henry Blofeld, the next I wasn't. I hadn't hit it terribly hard. But just to make sure it was broken, I threw it around the room a few times. Yes, it was broken all right.

This improved my sleep, but turned every subsequent morning into a wild search for cricket-related information. At the time my TV didn't have Ceefax, so that wasn't any use. There was no way of phoning up freelance friends who might have stayed up all night watching it on Sky, as they never surfaced before midday. Newspapers only ever reported the first few overs of the night ('Atherton survives Reid burst'), which left the TV news. And the ridiculous thing about TV news is that they never know which news is important and which news isn't. Serious difficulties on the M25? So what? Major in new EC yoghurt-lake initiative? Fine, but what's the bloody Test score?

It soon became apparent that Sky Sports had much to commend it, but my own facile snobbery prevented me from investing in a dish. I therefore became a cricket vampire, ringing up friends with dishes at odd times of the day and inviting myself around for a late-night drink or an early breakfast, whether or not they wanted me to come. I had no shame. I came out only in the hours of twilight, to suck the lifeblood out of people's satellite systems. They might have wanted to watch MTV, but they had not reckoned with my determination or indeed my valuable talent for laying hands on a late-night six-pack.

Wives barred me; girlfriends shunned me; strategically switched-on answering machines could not deter me. If there was cricket to be seen, I was there to see it. In the end, I had a stark choice: get a dish or cable system of my own, or forget about a social life for the rest of my days.

Nowadays it is almost impossible to imagine life before Charles Colvile, which is a grim thought in itself. Grotesque though satellite television is, it cannot be denied that Sky's blanket coverage of overseas Test matches has greatly enhanced our lives. I succumbed late, and I still resent the outrageous sums demanded of me – not least because as soon as you give in and hand over your life savings to Rupert Murdoch, your immediate reward is to discover what Bob Willis has been doing all these years. Because I only bought cable for the sports channel, and the only sport I watch on cable is cricket, I am effectively paying £22.99 a month for Bob Willis. 'Any thoughts of an Australian victory have gone up in smoke,' he said on 30 January 1995, 'and that smoke has come from the fire of Devon Malcolm.' No one should have to listen to this at 6.30 in the morning while still waiting for the kettle to boil. If someone takes a catch and Bob Willis is commentating, you *know* he is going to say: 'And Mark Waugh . . .' (short pause) '. . . made no mistake.' You know that the short pause was an attempt to think of something else to say, because he knows that he always says 'made no mistake'. Sometimes he says 'made no mistake' with real enthusiasm, as though he thinks that if he sounds lively people will think he has said something different. Or perhaps he genuinely thinks he has said something different, only subsiding into his usual torpor when he realises he has just said 'made no mistake' again.

And yet it is amazing what you can get used to. I speak, of course, of the small white silhouette of a duck which Sky Sports and its spiritual parent Channel 9 use to illustrate that a batsman has been dismissed without scoring. A dozen years ago this caused most British viewers to suffer spontaneous internal haemorrhages, often followed by long spells in hospital. Nowadays we barely notice it. Perhaps, in time, we can also get used to Bob Willis. I'm not sure I necessarily want to, but the possibility must at least be acknowledged.

Outside the rain is still pouring down. Sleet is due before the evening is out. There are months and months of this to go, during which England will lose another Test series, people will call for a complete overhaul of the game, the captain's position will be discussed, the manager's position will be discussed, the selectors' positions will be discussed, the counties will say that everything is all right at their end, and nothing will happen. Now you can see why hedgehogs hibernate.

CHAPTER EIGHTEEN

The Greatest Game

Every team has its greatest game. After a few seasons, unless you are a very sad person indeed, most memories of past matches melt into each other, and you can't quite remember who did what where and when and, in some cases, with whom. But the greatest game stands out, and everyone remembers it, whether or not they were there at the time. Even bad cricketers need folklore, but then even bad cricketers can exceed their brief to such a heroic extent that folklore spontaneously comes into being. That was certainly the case with the Captain Scott Invitation XI's greatest game, which survives as an anecdote only slightly more baroque than the day itself. It is hard to improve on reality.

Our greatest game took place at Marsh Gibbon, Buckinghamshire, on 29 April 1984. It was the first game of the season, against opponents who had tested us severely on previous occasions, partly by dint of their innate superiority, and partly because their pitch was situated on an unusually bleak plateau which allowed for no shelter against the prevailing weather conditions. In one early game it was so cold out there that everyone fielded in overcoats and Terence wore his balaclava (see Chapter 5). On this occasion, according to the team's journals, 'The match took place in unusually beautiful weather ... with only a gentle gale blowing and no buildings substantially damaged.' Nonetheless, we were cautiously optimistic about the outcome. Ours was undoubtedly a strong team – not least because, as we realised when we reached the ground, there were in fact twelve of us. If talent can't do it, sheer numbers can sometimes prevail. Fortunately, Marsh Gibbon also had an extra player to call upon, so after much grovelling for forgiveness on our part, the captains agreed to play twelve-a-side.

The Gibbon, as probably only we call them, won the toss and elected to bat. My friend Gags, who in those days could probably remember why he had been given such a ridiculous nickname, had been bowling like Dennis Lillee in the nets during most of March and April, but now bowled more like Dennis Lillee's grandmother. His fellow 'fast' bowlers delivered their long hops and half-volleys as though they had been practising them for months. Runs flowed with frustrating ease. Patrick, our captain, therefore removed these broken reeds and attempted to staunch the

flow with the off-spin of the striving young satirist and
Neal's dibbly-dobblies. This worked for a while but, as so
often, not quite long enough. By the time our official best
player had come on and rescued us with a timely 3 for
14, the ball had visited many parts of the neighbouring
countryside. On one such expedition, it landed on what
appeared to be a thick crust of dried mud, but was in
fact a cesspit. Our satirist leaped over the fence to retrieve
the ball, judging, incorrectly as it happens, that this crust
would take his weight. He recovered the ball all right,
but in the process immersed himself to the waist in the
source of all those good country smells. His team-mates
guffawed sympathetically as he trooped off for the first of
several showers. All refused to field downwind of him for
the remainder of the match.

At tea Marsh Gibbon declared at 146 for 5, and we
trudged into the pavilion in an oddly hopeful mood. I
myself was heard to utter the following portentous words:
'If we get a good start, we could win this.'

Harry and I were opening the batting, continuing an
experiment that had started successfully at the end of the
previous season. Slow and pedestrian though we undoubtedly were, we had both developed a facility for seeing off
the fast bowlers and then getting out, allowing the good
batsmen to come in and score some runs. That, however,
had been on fast August pitches, and 1983's summer had
been abnormally warm and bat-friendly. April at Marsh
Gibbon was a different proposition. Rawlings, the Gibbon's
strike bowler, walked back to his mark, which, after the
example of J.S.E. Price, was about four inches inside the

boundary. Perhaps it was the way he ran in at about 90 mph, or the way he bowled the ball at about double that, but we soon guessed that we were in trouble. Suddenly all the demons in the pitch which had lain dormant while we were bowling rose ominously to the surface. Harry, facing first, played and missed his way through a perilously fast over, which conceded 2 wides. The other bowler, thank God, was a little less fearsome; I played out a relatively untroubled maiden. More playing and missing from Harry, now looking justifiably nervous – until the third ball of the over leaped off a length and glanced against Harry's ear as he tried to pull away. Blood was visible. I gulped. The umpire, who was batting later, gulped. In the pavilion, everyone gulped as one. The next ball kept cruelly low, and Harry was bowled. He bled silently all the way back to pavilion. Next man in was the official best player, the advertising executive with humorous spectacles, who rarely lost his bottle but now looked ready to make an exception. The first ball he tried to edge to the wicketkeeper. The second ball he tried to edge to the wicketkeeper. The third ball he succeeded in edging to the wicketkeeper. Two for 2, with our official best player (main weakness: getting out in the forties) out for 0.

What was called for, of course, was a calm head to see off this demon and start playing for the draw that would surely be ours if one of the village's frequent hurricanes were to arrive before the scheduled close of play. Unfortunately, I was now facing, albeit against the lesser bowler, and I was a nervous wreck. I survived another maiden. Bill 'Chariots of Fire' Hoath played himself in against the dreaded Rawlings.

Still no runs off the bat. It was my third over against the other bowler. According to the report in the team's journal, 'Berkmann played a silly shot,' and as Berkmann wrote that report, I am inclined to take his word for it. Neal quickly followed. Two for 4; all four out for 0; highest scorer a Mr Wides.

In Rawlings' next over we finally scored a run. Unfortunately, in the process, we also lost 4 wickets. Chariots of Fire went first ball; then Chris Moore, soon to emigrate to Italy to get away from us, was bowled second ball by another daisy-cutter; and then the number 8 thumped his first ball down to long leg. Cheers rang out from the pavilion. The number 8 then ran himself out coming back for the second. At the other end the satirist, now in clean trousers, had been observing all this with shock and amazement, but had yet to face a ball. Rawlings bowled; satirist departed. From the relative prosperity of 2 for 4, we had slipped to 3 for 8. The first seven batsmen in the order had all been out for 0. Rawlings had taken 5 wickets for 1 run, and was removed from the attack.

Marsh Gibbon's captain now introduced a couple of donkey-droppers, and really you couldn't blame him. The late order took full advantage, and had raised the score to 7 by the time the 10th wicket fell. The 11th-wicket partnership did even better, for we finished on an almost respectable 16 all out, to lose by just 130 runs. The journal records that Patrick 'apologised to everyone concerned, and everyone said farewell to Marsh Gibbon for the last time'. In fact, seven years later they forgave us, and once again it became one of our most valued fixtures.

So why this match? Why not the no-less humiliating defeat against the Weekenders, six weeks later, when we were all out for 9? Why not any of the many gripping tussles against our old rivals at Charlton-on-Otmoor or Evenley? What made the Marsh Gibbon calamity unique, I think, was its potent combination of unfounded optimism (as reflected by our perky demeanour at the start of our innings) and blind abject panic (which set in five balls later). We felt that, for us, we weren't a bad side – and yet only the tiniest pressure needed to be applied before we fell apart. Between our aspirations and our achievements that day lay a void of almost interplanetary proportions. 'If we get a good start, we could win this.' That single sentence, awash in wide-eyed idiocy, somehow encapsulates the madness of cricket. That, and the fact that it only started to rain when we were on our way home.

BRAIN MEN

Marcus Berkmann

No need to phone a friend.

Who in the Bible killed a quarter of the world's population? What hardly ever happens in Hertford, Hereford or Hampshire? And what did Pink Floyd sing about once, Liza Minnelli twice and Abba three times?

The answers to these questions and more can be found in Brain Men, the ultimate insider's guide to scooping the £13.50 jackpot in your local pub. Quiz supremo Marcus Berkmann guides you through the type of trivia you need to win – the periodic table, shipping forecasts and international car stickers – whilst casting a wry look over quizzing origins, practices and unfortunate knitwear. In short, all human life is here, including the answer to question 6.

'Excellent . . . a Nick Hornby-influenced romp through the surreal world of the quiz buff'
Daily Mirror

'A hugely enjoyable book and you do not have to be interested in quizzes to love it'
Literary Review

'Marcus Berkmann can unlock that stash of useless facts lurking in your brain'
Guardian

Abacus
0 349 11299 1

UP NORTH

Charles Jennings

The North.

Where does it begin? Where does it end? And is it all whippets, black pudding, and queer folk going round saying 'There's nowt so queer as folk'?

Fresh from the P.J. O'Rourke School of Diplomatic Journalism, southern jessie Charles Jennings finds himself in need of Answers. With something approaching trepidation, Jennings packs his big girl's blouse in a suitcase full of prejudice and ventures fearfully into the great melting-pot that is the North of England – undergoing in the process a series of life changing experiences such as being mistaken for an exhibit at the Wigan Pier: Where History Comes Alive! Museum and voluntarily attending a concert featuring Roy Walker.

Scandalous, astonishingly rude, scabrously funny, *Up North* presents the quintessential northern experience.

'Jennings is blessed with a tremendous sense of humour and a gift for piercingly evocative prose . . . blissfully funny'
Sunday Telegraph

'He should have stayed under his duvet down south'
Mayor of Grimsby

'Very funny indeed . . . in the way that Bill Bryson was funny in
The Lost Continent'
Sunday Times

Abacus
0 349 10685 1

GENERATION X

Douglas Coupland

Andy, Dag and Claire have been handed a society priced beyond their means. Twentysomethings, brought up with divorce, Watergate and Three Mile Island, and scarred by the 80s fall-out of yuppies, recession, crack and Ronald Reagan, they represent the new lost generation – Generation X.

Fiercely suspicious of being lumped together as an advertiser's target market, they have quit dreary careers and cut themselves adrift in the California desert; in Palm Springs, land of the liposuction clinic and the shopping mall, dumping-ground for the dregs of American cultural memory.

Unsure of their futures, they immerse themselves in a regime of heavy drinking and working at McJobs – 'low-pay, low-prestige, low-benefit, no-future jobs in the service industry'. Underemployed, overeducated, intensely private and unpredictable, they have nowhere to direct their anger, no one to assuage their fears, and no culture to replace their anomie. So they tell stories; disturbingly funny tales that reveal their barricaded inner world. A world populated with dead TV shows, 'Elvis moments' and semi-disposable Swedish furniture . . .

'Riotous . . . a truly modern-day *Catcher in the Rye*'
Cosmopolitan

'A landmark book'
Daily Telegraph

'The overall effect is something close to a New Age
J.D. Salinger on smart drugs'
Time Out

Abacus
0 349 10839 0

Now you can order superb titles directly from Abacus

☐	Brain Men	Marcus Berkmann	£6.99
☐	Generation X	Douglas Coupland	£7.99
☐	Up North	Charles Jennings	£6.99
☐	Me Talk Pretty One Day	David Sedaris	£7.99

Please allow for postage and packing: **Free UK delivery.**
Europe; add 25% of retail price; Rest of World; 45% of retail price.

To order any of the above or any other Abacus titles, please call our credit card orderline or fill in this coupon and send/fax it to:

Abacus, P.O. Box 121, Kettering, Northants NN14 4ZQ
Tel: 01832 737527   Fax: 01832 733076
Email: aspenhouse@FSBDial.co.uk

☐ I enclose a UK bank cheque made payable to Abacus for £ ....

☐ Please charge £.............. to my Access, Visa, Delta, Switch Card No.

☐☐☐☐☐☐☐☐☐☐☐☐☐☐☐☐☐☐

Expiry Date ☐☐☐☐   Switch Issue No. ☐☐

NAME (Block letters please) ....

ADDRESS ....

....

....

Postcode ....Telephone ....

Signature ....

Please allow 28 days for delivery within the UK. Offer subject to price and availability.

Please do not send any further mailings from companies carefully selected by Abacus ☐